AMONG THE HUMORISTS
AND
AFTER-DINNER SPEAKERS

AMONG THE HUMORISTS
AND
AFTER-DINNER SPEAKERS

WILLIAM PATTEN

ISBN: 978-93-5420-016-8

Published: -

© 2020
LECTOR HOUSE LLP

LECTOR HOUSE LLP
E-MAIL: lectorpublishing@gmail.com

OLIVER HERFORD

AMONG THE HUMORISTS
AND
AFTER-DINNER SPEAKERS

A NEW COLLECTION OF
HUMOROUS STORIES AND ANECDOTES

SELECTED AND ARRANGED BY

WILLIAM PATTEN

Editor of American Short Story Classics, Foreign Short Story Classics, etc.

VOL. I.

PARTIAL LIST OF THE NAMES OF STORY-TELLERS IN THIS VOLUME

George Ade

Bret Harte

Mark Twain

Sec. of State P. C. Knox

W. M. Evarts

De Wolf Hopper

King Edward of England

Joseph Jefferson

Lord Beaconsfield

Abraham Lincoln

Alvey A. Adee

Patrick A. Collins

Horace T. Eastman

D. G. Rossetti

J. M. Maclaren

Dean Swift

Clyde Fitch

J. McNeill Whistler

Leigh Hunt

Edward Everett Hale

Dean Hole

Irving Bacheller

Thomas B. Reed

J. C. S. Blackburn

N. C. Goodwin

Brander Matthews

Andrew Carnegie

Speaker Cannon

Sir Wilfrid Laurier

Oliver Herford

J. M. Barrie

Richard Mansfield

John Sharp Williams

J. G. Blaine

Phillips Brooks

Daniel J. Sully

Bill Nye

John C. Spooner

Robert Edeson

Andrew Lang

Benjamin R. Tillman

William E. Gladstone

Charles Lamb

Edwin Booth

Weedon Grossmith

Senator W. A. Clark

Francis Wilson

Chauncey M. Depew

Albert J. Beveridge

Beerbohm Tree

Herbert S. Stone

Frank R. Stockton

Henry James

William Allen White

Bishop Brewster

Frederic Remington

Walter Damrosch

Rev. Robert Collyer

Rev. Sam Jones

Dean Kirchwey

John Wanamaker

Henry Guy Carleton

Charles Francis Adams

Julian Ralph

Senator John T. Morgan

J. J. Ingalls

Archbishop Ryan

J. A. Tawney

Thos. Bailey Aldrich

Elihu Root

PREFACE

THE *collection of these humorous paragraphs has extended over a number of years. Even a small beginning became a source of such entertainment that the collection grew and grew, always without any thought of publication.*

The man who can not laugh has yet to be found. Therein lies that immediate appeal to a common ground which the sense of humor gives, and it has been a conspicuous characteristic of those who look to the public for appreciation and support. Lord Palmerston and Abraham Lincoln were two notable examples of men for whom sympathy quickened through their ready wit, and no political speaker drives home his arguments half so well as he who can introduce a witty illustration. The joke has ever been a potent factor in combating oppression and corruption, in ridiculing shams. It has embalmed some reputations, and has blasted others. It is the champion of the weak against the strong, and has often illuminated for us, as in a flash, a glimpse of character or custom that would otherwise have been lost to the world.

There is only one similar collection of which I am aware, the "Jest Book" by Mark Lemon, who was for twenty-nine years the editor of "Punch." Alas that there should be fashions in jokes as well as in hats, for much of his book that we know must have been humorous reading to his contemporaries, leaves us, of the present generation in America, indifferent.

I shall be glad if some of my readers are minded to do a graceful act and send me, in return, some paragraphs to add to my collection.

I wish to take this opportunity to thank the following publications for the paragraphs borrowed from their columns:

Evening Sun, Lippincott's, Pittsburg Dispatch, San Francisco News-Letter, Ladies' Home Journal, Washington Star, Mail and Express, Youth's Companion, Life, Good Housekeeping, Argonaut, Buffalo Commercial, Tit-Bits, Punch, The Tattler, Harper's Weekly, Harper's Monthly, Democratic Telegram, Cleveland Plaindealer, Harvard Lampoon, Judge, Philadelphia Ledger, Saturday Evening Post, Philadelphia Evening Bulletin, Boston Herald, Kansas City Star, Washington Post, Success, Atchison Globe, New York Times, Woman's Home Companion, London Mail, Louisville Courier-Journal, Rochester Post-Express, New York Tribune, New York Observer, Chicago Daily News, Pittsburg Post, Pittsburg Observer, Philadelphia Public Ledger, New York World, Pick-me-up, Harper's Bazar, The Green Bag, Tacoma Ledger, Pittsburg Dispatch, The Wasp, Cornell Widow, Washington Post, Kansas City Independent, Short Stories.

W. P.

CONTENTS

AMONG THE HUMORISTS
AND AFTER-DINNER SPEAKERS

THERE is a delicious flavor about this story of a Virginia lady, married to a man who, though uniformly unsuccessful in his hunting trips, boastingly spoke of his "killings."

One day, returning from a trip, with the usual accompaniment of an empty bag, it occurred to him that his wife would make fun of him if he returned without even one proof of his oft-boasted skill. So he purchased a brace of partridges to deceive his trusting spouse. As he threw them on the table in front of her, he observed: "Well, my dear, you see I am not so awkward with the gun after all."

"Dick," replied the wife, turning from the birds with a grimace, after a brief examination, "you were quite right in shooting these birds to-day; to-morrow it would have been too late."

* * * * *

Uncle Toby was aghast at finding a strange darky with his arm around Mandy's waist.

"Mandy, tell dat niggah to take his ahm 'way from round yo' waist," he indignantly commanded. "Tell him yo'self," said Mandy haughtily. "He's a puffect stranger to me."

* * * * *

A Cockney tourist was on a visit to a Highland town famous for its golf-links. Through wearing a pair of stiff leather gaiters several sizes too large for him, he was compelled to walk bow-legged. Being a very slow player, others were forced to wait for him at every hole. At the fourth hole a Highlander after watching the visitor miss the ball three times was unable to wait any longer, and drove his ball clean between the tourist's legs. "What!" he of the gaitered legs yelled furiously. "Do you call that golf?" "Mebbe no," replied the Gael, "but it's very good croquet."

* * * * *

After the sermon on Sunday morning the rector welcomed and shook hands with a young German.

"And are you a regular communicant?" said the rector.

"Yes," said the German, "I take the 7.45 every morning."

* * * * *

Meeting a negro, a certain Southern gentleman asked him how he was getting on.

The negro assumed a troubled look, and replied:

"Oh, so far's physicality goes, I'm all right; but I sure do have ma troubles wif ma wife."

"Well, Sam, I'm sorry to hear that. What seems to be the matter?"

"She thinks money grows on trees, I reckon. All de time she keeps pesterin' me foh pinch o' change. If it ain't a dollah it's half or a quarter she wants."

"What on earth does she do with the money?"

"I dunno. Ain't nevah give her none yet."

* * * * *

A mountaineer of one of the back counties of North Carolina was arraigned with several others for illicit distilling. "Defendant," said the court, "what is your name?"

"Joshua," was the reply.

"Are you the man who made the sun stand still?"

Quick as a flash came the answer, "No, sir; I am the man who made the moon-shine."

* * * * *

"They thought more of the Legion of Honor in the time of the first Napoleon than they do now," said a well-known Frenchman. "The emperor one day met an old one-armed veteran.

"'How did you lose your arm?' he asked.

"'Sire, at Austerlitz.'

"'And were you not decorated?'

"'No, sire.'

"'Then here is my own cross for you; I make you chevalier.'

"'Your Majesty names me chevalier because I have lost one arm! What would your Majesty have done had I lost both arms?'

"'Oh, in that case I should have made you Officer of the Legion.'

"Whereupon the old soldier immediately drew his sword and cut off his other arm."

There is no particular reason to doubt this story. The only question is, how did he do it?

* * * * *

A stranger in Boston was interested to discover, when dining with friends once, that the dessert he would have classed as cream layer cake at home was known in Boston as "Washington pie." And the next time he lunched at a restaurant, he ordered the same thing; but the waiter put before him a rather heavy looking square of cake covered with chocolate, instead of the cream cake the guest had made up his mind to enjoy. A puzzled expression came over his face as he said reprovingly, "I ordered *Washington* pie, waiter."

"That is Washington pie, sir."

"Well," expostulated the disappointed man, "I did not mean Booker T.—I want *George!*"

* * * * *

George Ade, automobiling in Indiana, dined at a country hotel among a roomful of ministers.

The ministers, who were holding a convention in the town, were much amused when Mr. Ade's identity was disclosed to them.

One of them said during dinner:

"How does a humorist of your stamp feel, sir, in such reverend company as this?"

"I feel," said Mr. Ade promptly, "like a lion in a den of Daniels."

* * * * *

It was a crowded tram car. Among those who could not find seats was a young lady. Close to where she stood an old man was sitting. He struggled as if to rise. The young woman cast a glance of scorn at one or two men hiding behind newspapers. "Please don't get up," she said to the old man, "I beg you won't." The conductor rang the bell and the car went on. The old man's features worked convulsively and he mopped his face with his handkerchief. At the next stopping place he again tried to rise and again the young woman tried to stop him. "I would much rather stand," she said, continuing to block his way. "I don't care whether you would or not," said the old man, crimson with fury, "I want to get out. You've made me come half a mile too far already. Here, you, stop the car." But it was too late, the bell had already rung and he had to wait until the next stopping place was reached.

* * * * *

"I want some cigars for my husband for Christmas."

"What kind, madam?"

"Well, I don't know, exactly; but he is a middle-aged man and always dresses in black."

* * * * *

John D. Rockefeller, Jr., tells a story of his father:

"Father tells many stories. Sometimes he tells a new one. Not long ago he related one to me that concerned a man who had imbibed rather too freely. The man, in this condition, fell into a watering trough. To the officer who came to help him out as he wallowed in the water, he said:

"'Offzer, I ken save self. You save women an' shildern.'"

* * * * *

"On Sunday, September 20, the wife of — — of a daughter. Others please copy."

* * * * *

Bret Harte was so frequently complimented as the author of "Little Breeches" that he was almost as sorry it was ever written as was Colonel John Hay, who preferred his fame to rest on more ambitious works. A gushing lady who prided herself upon her literary tastes, said to him once: "My dear Mr. Harte, I am so delighted to meet you. I have read everything you ever wrote, but of all your dialect verse there is none that compares to your 'Little Breeches.'"

"I quite agree with you, madam," said Mr. Harte, "but you have put the little breeches on the wrong man."

* * * * *

Mr. Knox, the Secretary of State in Taft's Cabinet, was formerly engaged in the practise of law in Pittsburg.

One day, says a friend, Mr. Knox was much put out to find on his arrival at his office that everything was topsy-turvy and that the temperature of his rooms was much too low for comfort. Summoning his office-boy, a lad but recently entered his employ, the lawyer asked who had raised every window in the place on such a cold morning.

"Mr. Muldoon, sir," was the answer.

"Who is Mr. Muldoon?" asked the attorney.

"The janitor, sir."

"Who carried off my waste-basket?" was the next question.

"Mr. Reilly, sir."

"And who is Mr. Reilly?"

"He's the man that cleans the rooms."

Mr. Knox looked sternly at the boy and said: "See here, Richard, we call men by their first names here. We don't 'mister' them in this office. Do you understand?"

"Yes, sir." And the boy retired.

In a few minutes he reappeared and in a shrill, piping voice announced:

"There's a gentleman that wants to see you, Philander."

* * * * *

A Scottish parson, still on the under side of forty, was driving home from an outlying hamlet when he overtook a young woman. He recognized her as the maid of all work at a farm which he would pass, so he pulled up and offered her a lift. Mary gladly accepted his offer and they chatted pleasantly all the way to the farm gate.

"Thank you, sir," she said as she got down.

"Don't mention it, Mary. Don't mention it," he told her politely.

"No, I won't," Mary obligingly assured him.

* * * * *

A little girl was shown her newly-arrived baby brother. Looking at him lovingly she said, "When will he talk, mother?" "Oh not for a long time yet," said the mother. "Yes, but when?" persisted the child. "Well, not for a year or so." After thinking for minute the child exclaimed, "How funny. Miss Clark read out of the Bible this morning that Job cursed the hour he was born."

* * * * *

W. A. Sponsler, when in the Pennsylvania State Legislature, was given to the making of very elaborate and florid speeches, and one day brought an address to a close with "*Vox populi, vox Dei.*"

"I'll bet you don't know the meaning of what Sponsler just said," said Al Crawford to Hugh E. Mackin.

"I don't know!" replied Mackin, indignantly. "Of course, I know!"

"You don't know for ten dollars!" suggested Crawford.

Mackin, still indignant, posted his part of the wager with another member of the Legislature, and Crawford said tauntingly:

"Well, now, tell us, what does it mean?"

"*Vox populi, vox Dei,*" quoted Mackin, solemnly, "as everybody knows, is French for 'My God! why hast thou forsaken me?'"

"Give him the money," said Crawford. "Darned if he don't know after all!"

* * * * *

There is an old lady living in a small town in southern Pennsylvania who makes great efforts to keep abreast of the times. Her opportunities, however, are circumscribed, and she is sometimes compelled to resort to her imagination. She went to a church sociable lately, and as she entered the room one of the attendants said:

"Good evening, auntie. I am glad you came. We are going to have tableaux this evening."

"Yes, I know," replied the old lady; "I smelt 'em when I first came in."

* * * * *

Fifer was a dog of friendly and social habits, but when he wandered into the lecture-tent at a well-known New Thought summer school and went to sleep between the chairs, he did a very foolish thing. A woman coming in poked him in the ribs with her parasol, startling him from his peaceful dreams, and he sprang upon her with a savage bite. A man grabbed him and he grabbed the man. The excitement was intense when an earnest little woman standing on a chair cried, "Some one hold the Thought!" "Hang the Thought!" shouted a man in the rear. "Some one hold the dog!"

* * * * *

The boy was going away to school, full of high hope.

"I shall make the football team and color two pipes the first year!" he said bravely.

His mother kissed him and wept. His father wrung his hand in silence.

They were too full for speech then.

But when he was gone, and they were calmer, they talked together of him, and prayed his ambition might not carry him beyond his strength.

* * * * *

The car was entirely empty with the exception of one man, but as I entered he rose, made me an unsteady but magnificent bow, and said: "Madam, pleashe be kind 'nough to asshept thish plashe."

There was nothing else for me to do, so I thanked him and sat down. And for twenty blocks that idiot hung from a strap, swaying in the breeze, with not a soul in the car but ourselves. Occasionally I have been taken for other women; but I never before had any one think that I was a carful.

* * * * *

Husband (after the theater) — "Well, how do you like the piece?"

Wife — "Very much. There's only one improbable thing in it. The second act takes place two years after the first, and they have the same servant."

* * * * *

Thomas Hill (the original "Paul Pry") was endeavoring one evening to cut up an orange in such a fashion as to represent a pig. After strewing the table with about a dozen peels, he gave up the futile experiment, saying, "Hang the pig! I can't make him at all."

"Nonsense, Hill," said Theodore Hook, pointing to the table; "you have done splendidly. Instead of a pig you have made a litter."

* * * * *

An elderly churchwarden in shaving himself one Sunday before church-time made a slight cut with the razor on the extreme end of his nose. Quickly calling to his wife, he asked her if she had any court-plaster in the house. "You will find some in my sewing basket," she said. The warden soon had the cut covered. At church in assisting with the collection he noticed everyone smile as he passed the plate, and some of the younger people laughed outright. Very much annoyed, he asked a friend if there was anything wrong with his appearance. "Well, I should think there is," was the answer. "What is that on your nose?" "Court-plaster." "No," said his friend, "it is the label from a reel of cotton. It says, 'Warranted 200 yd. long.'"

* * * * *

A man who stuttered very badly went to a specialist, and after ten difficult lessons learned to say quite distinctly, "Peter Piper picked a peck of pickled peppers." His friends congratulated him upon this splendid achievement.

"Yes," said the man, doubtfully, "but it's s-s-such a d-d-deucedly d-d-d-difficult rem-mark to w-work into an ordin-n-nary c-c-convers-s-sa-tion, y' know."

* * * * *

Toastmaster (to chairman of public dinner) — "Would you like to propose your toast now, my lord, or should we let 'em enjoy themselves a bit longer?"

* * * * *

A visitor to a Sunday-school was asked to address a few remarks to the children. He took the familiar theme of the children who mocked Elisha on his journey to Bethel — how the youngsters taunted the poor old prophet and how they were punished when two she bears came out of the wood and ate forty-and-two of them. "And now, children," said he, wishing to learn if his talk had produced any moral effect, "what does this story show?" "Please, sir," came from a little girl well down in the front, "it shows how many children two she bears can hold."

* * * * *

A curate who had left his parish on account of the attentions of his lady parishioners, meeting his successor one day in the street asked him how he got on in his new position. "Very well indeed," returned the other. "But are not the ladies rather pressing in their attentions?" "Oh, my dear fellow, I manage that all right, I find safety in Numbers." "I see," returned his companion, "well, I found safety in Exodus."

* * * * *

"I want some collars for my husband," said a lady in a department store, "but I am afraid I have forgotten the size."

"Thirteen and a half, ma'am?" suggested the clerk.

"That's it. How on earth did you know?"

"Gentlemen who let their wives buy their collars for 'em are almost always about that size, ma'am," explained the observant clerk.

* * * * *

On a recent occasion before leaving Marlborough House new clothes were ordered for Prince Edward, and according to custom a tailoress was sent to fit him at a time which would not interfere with his lessons. The tailoress duly arrived and was ushered to the Prince's sitting-room, but on the door being opened she paused as she saw that a gentleman, whose face was turned toward the fireplace, was sitting smoking and chatting with the children. Prince Edward, whose manner is most friendly, at once ran forward and told her to come in, and seeing that she still hesitated added in a reassuring voice, "You needn't mind, it's only grandpapa."

* * * * *

A physician engaged a nurse, recently graduated, for a case of delirium tremens. The physician succeeded in quieting his patient and left some medicine, instructing the nurse to administer it to him if he "began to see snakes again." At the next call the physician found the patient again raving. To his puzzled inquiry the nurse replied that the man had been going on that way for several hours, and that she had not given him any medicine.

"But didn't I tell you to give it to him if he began to see snakes again?" asked the physician.

"But he didn't see snakes this time," replied the nurse confidently. "He saw red, white, and blue turkeys with straw hats on."

* * * * *

Shortly after his entrance into political life Disraeli stood for a certain Middlesex borough in the Conservative interest. It was a "personally conducted" canvass, and, among others, the future Prime Minister solicited the vote and interest of a well-to-do but somewhat irascible farmer, who was supposed to be rather doubtful in his political convictions.

"Vote for you!" he shouted when Mr. Disraeli made known the object of his call. "Why, I'd vote for the devil sooner."

"Ah, quite so!" said Mr. Disraeli, suavely, "but in event of your friend not standing, may I hope for your interest?"

* * * * *

An ambitious youth once sent his first MS. to Dumas, asking the distinguished novelist to become his *collaborateur*. The latter was astounded at the impertinence. Angrily seizing his pen, he wrote: "How dare you, sir, yoke together a noble horse and a contemptible ass?"

He received the following reply:

"How dare you sir, call me a horse?"

His anger vanished and he laughingly penned the following:

"Send on your MS., my friend; I gladly accept your proposition."

* * * * *

An old farmer recently came into possession of a check for $200. He finally summoned up nerve enough to go to the bank.

"What denomination?" said the teller, hastily, as the check was passed in through the window.

"Luther'n, gol darn it. But what has that got to do with it?"

* * * * *

A young woman was in company with a university graduate, and naturally the talk ran upon books. By and by there was a lull in the conversation, broken presently by the young woman, who said: "What do you think of Fielding, Mr. Smith?"

"Oh," was the answer, "fielding is important, of course; but it isn't worth much unless you have good pitching and batting."

* * * * *

General Frederick D. Grant said to his servant one morning: "James, I have left my mess boots out. I want them soled."

"Yes, sir," the servant answered.

The general, dressing for dinner that night, said again:

"I suppose, James, that you did as I told you about those boots?"

James laid thirty-five cents on the bureau.

"Yes, sir," said he, "and this is all I could get for them, though the corporal who bought 'em said he'd have given half a dollar if pay day hadn't been so far off."

* * * * *

President Lincoln once wrote to General McClellan, when the latter was in command of the army. General McClellan, as is well known, conducted a waiting campaign, being so careful not to make any mistakes that he made very little headway. President Lincoln sent this brief but exceedingly pertinent letter:

> "*My dear McClellan*: If you don't want to use the army I should like to borrow it for a while.

> "Yours respectfully,
> "A. Lincoln."

* * * * *

It was at a children's party in West Kensington. The youngsters had just done more than justice to the luxurious spread provided by their hostess, and games were now the order of the evening.

"Now, children," said she, "we will play the zoo, and each of you must represent a different animal."

Then, going to a little girl, she asked:

"Now, Carrie, what are you going to be?"

"I'll be an elephant."

"And you, Reggie, what are you going to be?"

"I'm going to be a lion."

"And what are you going to be, Hilda?"

"I'm going to be a tiger."

Then, crossing to the other side of the room, the hostess, noticing a youngster sitting all alone, asked:

"And what are you going to be, Tommy?"

"P-please," was the halting reply, "p-please—I'm going—to be sick."

* * * * *

A man who had been convicted of stealing was brought before a certain "down East" judge, well known for his tender-heartedness, to be sentenced.

"Have you ever been sentenced to imprisonment?" asked the judge, not unkindly.

"Never!" exclaimed the prisoner, suddenly bursting into tears.

"Well, well, don't cry, my man," said his honor consolingly; "you're going to be now."

* * * * *

The inventor of a new feeding bottle for infants sent out the following among his directions for using:

"When the baby is done drinking it must be unscrewed and laid in a cool place under the hydrant. If the baby does not thrive on fresh milk, it should be boiled."

* * * * *

A well-known New York clergyman was telling his Bible class the story of the Prodigal Son at a recent session, and wishing to emphasize the disagreeable attitude of the elder brother on that occasion, he laid especial stress on this phase of the parable. After describing the rejoicing of the household over the return of the wayward son, he spoke of one who, in the midst of the festivities, failed to share in the jubilant spirit of the occasion.

"Can anybody in the class," he asked, "tell me who this was?"

A small boy, who had been listening sympathetically to the story, put up his hand.

"I know," he said, beamingly; "it was the fatted calf."

* * * * *

"I understand," said the old-time friend, "that you are gettin' right exclusive."

"Well," answered Mr. Cumrox, "that's what mother an' the girls call it."

"What do you call it?"

"Plain 'lonesome'."

* * * * *

"Tommy," said the hostess, "you appear to be in deep thought."

"Yes'm," replied Tommy; "ma told me somethin' to say if you should ask me to have some cake or anything, an' I bin here so long now I forgit what it was."

* * * * *

A Boston minister once noticed a crowd of urchins clustered around a dog of doubtful pedigree.

"What are you doing, my little men?" he asked with fatherly interest.

"Swappin' lies," volunteered one of the boys. "The feller that tells the biggest one gets the purp."

"Shocking!" exclaimed the minister. "Why, when I was your age I never even *thought* of telling an untruth."

"Youse win," chorused the urchins. "The dog's yours, mister."

* * * * *

A Brooklyn Sunday-school teacher once had occasion to catechise a new pupil whose ignorance of his Testament would have been amusing had it not been so appalling. One Sunday she asked the little fellow how many commandments there were.

To her surprise, the lad answered, glibly enough: "Ten, ma'am."

"And now, Sammy," pleasantly asked the teacher, "what would the result be if you should break one of them?"

"Then there'd be nine!" triumphantly answered the youngster.

* * * * *

William J. Carr, of the State Department, had occasion to call at the house of a neighbor late at night. He rang the door-bell. After a long wait a head was poked out of a second-floor window.

"Who's there?" asked a voice.

"Mr. Carr," was the reply.

"Well," said the voice as the window banged shut, "what do I care if you missed a car? Why don't you walk, and not wake up people to tell them about it?"

* * * * *

A clever veterinary has a system all his own. When he received an overfed toy dog he would consign him to a disused brick oven, with a crust of bread, an onion and an old boot. When the dog began to gnaw the bread, the anxious mistress was informed that her darling was "doing nicely." When it commenced operation on the onion, word was sent that the pet was "decidedly better"; but when the animal tackled the boot, my lady was gratified to hear that her precious pet was "ready to be removed."

* * * * *

A lady while going downstairs to dinner had the misfortune to step slightly on the dress of a lady in front of her. The man on whose arm the former was leaning rudely said aloud so that the couple in front might hear, "Always getting in the way like Balaam's ass!" Upon which the lady whose gown had been trodden on, turning round, replied with a sweet smile, "Pardon me, it was the angel who stood in the way and the ass which spoke."

* * * * *

A number of years ago, when the former Second Assistant Secretary of State, Alvey A. Adee, was Third Assistant, an employee of the State Department was called to the 'phone.

"Will you kindly give me the name of the Third Assistant Secretary of State?" asked the voice at the other end of the wire.

"Adee."

"A. D. what?"

"A. A. Adee."

"Spell it, please."

"A."

"Yes."

"A."

"Yes."

"A— —"

"You go to the d— —!" and the receiver was indignantly hung up.

* * * * *

Smith and Jones, talking about the Kaiser:

Jones—"They tell me that unfortunately he is very bellicose."

Smith—"Dear me! You surprise me! I always understood he was rather tall and slim."

* * * * *

"I will be your valentine," said the young man.

A shadow passed across the fair face of the girl. "I was so in hopes that I would not get any comics this year," she said.

* * * * *

One of the favorite stories of Mayor Collins of Boston was about a man who, accompanied by his little boy, had occasion to cross a lot where a good-sized goat was feeding.

The father was a Christian Scientist and always carried a copy of Mrs. Eddy's works in his pocket. As they approached the goat the boy showed fear, whereat his father told him to think it not possible for the animal to harm them, but the boy, remembering a previous encounter with a goat, in which he came out second best, did not grow any braver.

"Papa, you're a Christian Scientist, all right," he said, "and so am I; but the goat doesn't know it."

* * * * *

Horace T. Eastman, the inventor of the locomotive pilot, said the other day:

"This morning I was sitting in a drug store waiting to get a prescription filled when a young Irishman entered.

"The Irishman pointed to a stack of green Castile soap and said:

"'Oi want a lump o' thot.'

"'Very well, sir,' said the clerk. 'Will you have it scented or unscented?'

"'Oi'll take ut with me,' said the Irishman."

* * * * *

Robert Smith, brother of Sydney Smith, and an ex-Advocate-General, on one occasion engaged in an argument with a physician over the relative merits of their respective professions.

"I don't say that all lawyers are crooks," said the doctor, "but you'll have to admit that your profession doesn't make angels of men."

"No," retorted Smith; "you doctors certainly have the best of us there."

* * * * *

Small chap—"Say, papa, what is the race problem?"

Papa—"Picking winners."

* * * * *

The temperance society was to meet that afternoon. Mrs. Philpots dressed in a hurry and came panting downstairs. She was a short, plump woman.

"Addie, run up to my room and get my blue ribbon rosette, the temperance badge," she directed her maid. "I have forgotten it. You will know it, Addie—blue ribbon and gold lettering."

"Yas'm, I knows it right well." Addie could not read, but she knew a blue ribbon with gold lettering when she saw it, and therefore had no trouble in finding it and fastening it properly on the dress of her mistress.

Mrs. Philpots was too busy greeting her friends or giving close attention to the speakers at the meeting to note that they smiled when they shook hands with her.

When she reached home, supper was served, so she went directly to the dining-room, where the other members of the family were seated.

"Gracious me, mother!" exclaimed her son. "That blue ribbon—have you been wearing that at the temperance meeting?"

A loud laugh went up on all sides.

"Why, what is it, Harry?" asked the good woman, clutching at the ribbon in surprise.

"Why, mother, dear, didn't you know that was the ribbon I wore at the show?"

The gold lettering on the ribbon read:

Atlanta Poultry Show.

First Prize.   Bantam.

* * * * *

At a dinner party recently given the subject of regular hours and plain diet was discussed. Several had spoken when one of the guests remarked, "You may not believe it, but for ten years I rose on the stroke of six, half an hour later was at breakfast, at seven was at work, dined at one, had supper at six, and was in bed at 9.30. In all that time I ate the plainest food and did not have a day's sickness." The silence that followed was awful, but finally another guest asked, "Will you permit a question?" "Certainly," was the reply; "what do you wish to know?" "Well, just out of curiosity," said the other, "I would like to know what you were in prison for?"

* * * * *

Watch—"Eight bells, and all's well!"

Mrs. Pohunk (feebly)—"I guess, Josiah, he hasn't looked on this side of the boat lately or he'd know better."

* * * * *

When the minister, who was a bachelor, had been helped to Mrs. Porter's biscuits for the third time, he looked across the table at Rhoda, staring at him with round, wondering eyes.

"I don't often have such a good supper as this, my dear," he said, in his most propitiatory tone, and Rhoda's face dimpled.

"We don't, always," she said, in her clear little voice. "I'm awful glad you came."

* * * * *

The late Charles Matthews now and then failed, like some of the rest of us, in meeting his bills as promptly as the tradespeople concerned could desire.

On one occasion a brisk young tailor, named Berry, lately succeeded to his father's business, sent in his account somewhat ahead of time.

Whereupon Matthews, with virtuous rage, seized his pen and wrote him the following note:

"You must be a goose—Berry, to send me your bill—Berry, before it is due—Berry.

"Your father, the elder—Berry, would have had more sense.

"You may look very black—Berry, and feel very blue—Berry, but I don't care a straw—Berry, for you and your bill—Berry."

* * * * *

A clergyman in a Lawrence church on a recent occasion discovered, after beginning the service, that he had forgotten his notes. As it was too late to send for them, he said to his audience, by way of apology, that this morning he should have to depend upon the Lord for what he might say, but in the afternoon he would come better prepared.

* * * * *

An American visiting London for the first time, goaded to desperation by the incessant necessity for tips, finally entered the wash-room of his hotel, only to be faced with a large sign which read: "Please tip the basin after using." "I'm hanged if I will!" said the Yankee, turning on his heel, "I'll go dirty first!"

* * * * *

Mother could not attend church one Sunday. "But what a shame that little Mabel should have to lose the day's lesson, and she *such* a bright child," she sadly reflected. Accordingly, Mabel was sent alone. When she returned, in reply to her mother's interrogation as to the subject of the text, she replied, "Oh, yes, mother, I know; it was *'Don't get scared: You'll get the quilt.'*" Questioning failed to throw any light on the matter. Some days later the mother met the pastor, who, in answer to her request for the subject of his last sermon, replied, "It was, madam, 'Fear not: Ye shall have the Comforter.'"

* * * * *

Mark Twain in his lecturing days, reached a small Eastern town one afternoon and went before dinner to a barber's to be shaved.

"You are a stranger in town, sir?" the barber asked.

"Yes, I am a stranger here," was the reply.

"We're having a good lecture here to-night, sir," said the barber, "a 'Mark Twain' lecture. Are you going to it?"

"Yes, I think I will," said Mr. Clemens.

"Have you got your ticket yet?" the barber asked.

"No, not yet," said the other.

"Then, sir, you'll have to stand."

"Dear me!" Mr. Clemens exclaimed. "It seems as if I always do have to stand when I hear that man Twain lecture."

* * * * *

During the visit of the Shah Nasr-ed-Din to England he dined one night with the then Prince of Wales, now King Edward. Among the courses was one of asparagus, a delicacy unknown to the Shah. He considered it for a time, discovered that the head alone was nice to eat, ate it accordingly and flung the rest of the stalk over his shoulder. The other diners were somewhat flabbergasted, but the tactful Prince, not wishing his Persian guest to feel that he had done anything ridiculous, promptly followed his example, throwing his own stalks over his shoulder. Naturally all the courtiers imitated him in turn, and the amazement of the royal servants was extreme to see the air suddenly full of flying asparagus stalks from one end of the lengthy room to the other.

* * * * *

On one of his frequent trips to the other side, the weather being more than ordinarily rough, and the passengers on deck but few, the late Bishop Potter saw a lady reclining on one of the benches, and the unearthly pallor on her face and the hapless languidity of her manner indicated that she had reached that state of collapse which marks the limit of sea-sickness. "Touched by this piteous spectacle and approaching the poor creature, in my most compassionate tone I asked, 'Madam, can I be of any service to you?'

"She did not open her eyes, but I heard her murmur faintly: 'Thank you, sir, but there is nothing you can do—nothing at all.' 'At least, madam,' said I tenderly, 'permit me to bring you a glass of water.' She moved her head feebly and answered: 'No, I thank you—nothing at all.' 'But your husband, madam,' said I, 'the gentleman lying there with his head in your lap—shall I not bring something to revive him?' The lady again moved her head feebly, and again she murmured faintly between gasps: 'Thank you, sir, but—he—is—not—my—husband. I—don't—know—who he is!'"

* * * * *

"Well, Bobby, how do you like church?" asked his father, as they walked homeward from the sanctuary, to which Bobby had just paid his first visit.

"It's fine," ejaculated the young man. "How much did you get, father?"

"How much did I get? Why, what do you mean? How much what?" asked the parent, astonished at this evident irreverence.

"Why, don't you remember when the funny old man passed the money around? I only got ten cents."

* * * * *

One day a fussy fellow met Father Healy of Dublin by the seashore and thus accosted him: "Father Healy, I am undergoing a cure, and I take a tumbler of sea water three times a day. Now, I've had my full allowance to-day, but do you think I might have one, just one, tumbler more?"

Father Healy put his head on one side and looked at the ocean, lost in thought. "Well," he said, at last, with a gravely judicial air, "I don't think it would be missed."

* * * * *

Wm. M. Evarts asked by a lady if he did not think that woman was the best judge of woman, he replied: "Not only the best judge, madam, but the best executioner."

* * * * *

De Wolf Hopper was calling down a speaking-tube to the janitor of his apartment in New York. Mr. Hopper, unable to get the information he desired, finally blurted out, "Say, is there a blithering idiot at the end of this tube?" The reply came back with startling rapidity, "Not at this end, sir."

* * * * *

Mrs. S.—"Surely, John, you haven't brought anyone home to dinner?"

Mr. S.—"Sure I have. Haven't you got anything for them?"

"Why no, you told me you'd bring home a couple of lobsters for dinner."

"So I have, they're in the parlor."

* * * * *

One of his grandma's maids of honor tells the following story of Prince Eddie when he was a few years younger:

Just after King Edward's coronation, when he underwent an operation for appendicitis and was lying convalescent, he sent for his grandchildren.

The little ones trooped into the room, cautioned by their nurse that they must keep very quiet, and stood about their grandfather's bed. He talked with them for a few minutes and they replied in awed whispers. Then when the nurse told them they must go, Prince Eddie said:

"But, grandpa, can't we see the baby?"

* * * * *

Rossetti's fondness for humorous stories and his interest in a particular soldier of fortune, or rather of misfortune, are shown in Hall Caine's autobiography. Beginning life as the secretary of Ruskin, the man ultimately lived on his cleverness and audacity and made Rossetti in particular his conscious and delighted victim. Feeble as Rossetti was, the visits of this man did him good, and he laughed all the evening and told droll stories himself. One of the latter was of a man near to death to whom the clergyman came and said: "Dear friend, do you know who died to save you?" "Oh, meenister, meenister," said the dying man, "is this a time for conundrums?"

* * * * *

It is interesting to recall, apropos of the recent Milton celebration, an anecdote of Milton that was told in an old family letter written in 1762, recently quoted in the columns of the London "Spectator":

"Possibly you may not have heard this anecdote concerning him. John Vallack—who, I believe, died after you came to Tavistock—told me it, and he lived in London in 1696. Milton, as you know, was blind. Charles the Second had the curiosity to see him, and said: 'God hath punished you for your malice, etc., to my father by taking away your eyesight.'

"'Aye,' says Milton, 'but before I lost my eyes he lost his head.'"

* * * * *

In writing a sketch of Washington a pupil ended her essay by saying: "Washington married a famous belle, Martha Custis, and in due time became the father of his country."

* * * * *

A certain regiment was on the march from Philadelphia to Gettysburg and the companies were ordered to move with a few minutes' interval between them and to keep each other in sight, the band and drums leading.

The band soon got a long way ahead, and on reaching a bend, halted for a few minutes' rest. Presently up galloped a mounted officer in hot haste and shouted for the band sergeant.

"What do you mean," he said, "by getting out of sight of the leading company?"

"We were not out of sight, sir," answered the sergeant.

"What do you mean by telling me that!" exclaimed the officer in a rage. "You were out of sight, I saw you myself."

* * * * *

Several ladies sat after a card party at the University Club a few mornings ago, discussing the virtues of their husbands. "Mr. Bingleton," said one of them, referring to her life partner, "never drinks and never swears—indeed, he has no bad habits." "Does he ever smoke?" some one asked. "Yes; he likes a cigar just after he has eaten a good meal. But, I suppose, on an average, he doesn't smoke more than once a month."

* * * * *

Ian Maclaren was talking to a group of literary beginners in New York. "Begin your stories well," he said emphatically. "There's nothing like a good beginning. Indeed, it's half the battle." Then with a smile this excellent beginner of stories added: "Always bear in mind the case of the young man who, desiring to marry, secured a favorable hearing from his sweetheart's irascible father by opening the interview with the words: 'I know a way, sir, whereby you can save money.'"

* * * * *

Benevolent gentleman—"My little boy, have you no better way to spend this beautiful afternoon than by standing in front of the gate, idling away your time?"

Boy—"I ain't idling away my time. There's a chump inside with my sister, who is paying me ten cents an hour to watch for pa."

* * * * *

That famous Scotch physician, Dr. George Fordyce, was unfortunately somewhat given to drink, and though he never was known to be dead drunk, yet he was often in a state which rendered him unfit for professional duties. One night when he was in such a condition, he was suddenly sent for to attend a lady of title who was very ill. He went, sat down, listened to her story, and felt her pulse. He found he was not up to his work. He lost his wits and in a moment of forgetfulness exclaimed, "Drunk, by Jove!" Still he managed to write out a mild prescription. Early next morning he received a message from the noble patient to call on her at once. Dr. Fordyce felt very uncomfortable. The lady evidently intended to upbraid him either for giving an improper prescription or for his disgraceful condition, but to his surprise and relief she thanked him for his prompt compliance with her pressing summons, and then confessed that he had rightly diagnosed her case. That unfortunately she occasionally indulged too freely in drink, but that she hoped he would preserve inviolable secrecy as to the condition in which he had found her. Fordyce listened to her as grave as a judge, then said:

"Madam, you may depend on me. I shall be as silent as the grave."

* * * * *

A friend of Dean Swift one day sent him a turbot as a present by a servant lad who had frequently been on similar errands but had never received anything from the dean for his trouble. Having gained admission he opened the study door, and putting down the fish on the floor cried out rudely, "Master has sent you a turbot." "Young man," said the dean rising from the chair, "is that the way you deliver a message? Let me teach you better manners. Sit down in my chair; we will change places, and I will show you how to behave in future." The boy sat down, and the dean going out came up to the door, and making a low bow said, "Sir, master presents his kind compliments, hopes you are well, and requests your acceptance of a small present." "Does he?" replied the boy. "Return him my best thanks, and there's half-a-crown for yourself." The dean thus caught in his own trap laughed heartily and gave the boy a crown for his ready wit.

* * * * *

A spunky little mule was trying to throw his darky rider and in kicking about caught his hoof in a stirrup, upon which the darky cried out in frightened tones, "Say, if you'se gwine to git on, I'se gwine to git off."

* * * * *

"I ought not to be surprised by anything at my time of life," said a well-known minister, "but one of my flock did manage to take my breath away. I was preaching about the Father's tender wisdom in caring for us all," he said. "I illustrated by saying that the Father knows which of us grows best in sunlight and which of us must have shade. 'You know you plant roses in the sunshine,' I said, 'and heliotrope and geraniums; but if you want your fuchsias to grow they must be kept in a shady nook.' After the sermon, which I hoped would be a comforting one, a woman came up to me, her face glowing with pleasure that was evidently deep and true. 'O, Dr. — —, I am so grateful for that sermon,' she said, clasping my hand and shaking it warmly. My heart glowed for a moment, while I wondered what tender place in her heart and life I had touched. Only for a moment, though. 'Yes,' she went on, fervently, 'I never knew before what was the matter with my fuchsias.'"

* * * * *

There are some singular discounts allowed in the book trade. They were happily illustrated on one occasion by Mark Twain. One day while the humorist was connected with a publishing house he went into a book store and picking up a volume asked the price. He then suggested that as a publisher he was entitled to 50 per cent discount. To this the clerk assented.

"As I am also an author," said Mark, "it would appear that I am again entitled to 50 per cent discount."

Again the clerk bowed.

"And as a personal friend of the proprietor," he modestly continued, "I presume that you will allow me the usual 25 per cent. discount."

Another bow from the salesman.

"Well," drawled the unblushing humorist, "under these conditions I think I may as well take the book. What's the tax?"

The clerk took out his pencil and figured industriously. Then he said with the greatest obsequiousness:

"As near as I can calculate we owe you the book and about 37½ cents."

* * * * *

Clyde Fitch tells a new story of Whistler. The artist was in Paris at the time of the coronation of King Edward, and at a reception one evening a duchess said to him: "I believe you know King Edward, Mr. Whistler."

"No, madame," replied Whistler.

"Why, that's odd," she murmured; "I met the King at a dinner-party last year, and he said that he knew you."

"Oh," said the painter, "that was just his brag."

* * * * *

A London friend who was a member of the same club as Mr. Whistler writes me this, which I have not seen before in print. It seems that the gentle artist in making enemies had not paid his dues and was dunned for them in vain. He either took no notice of requests for a settlement, or replied to them with his usual airy mockery. Finally the secretary wrote to him:

"*Dear Mr. Whistler* — It is not a Nocturne in Purple, or a Symphony in Blue and Gray, that we are after, but An Arrangement in Gold and Silver."

This drew forth the required pounds and shillings.

* * * * *

Here is another story typical of the great maker of enemies:

Whistler had a French poodle of which he was extravagantly fond. The poodle was seized with an affection of the throat, and Whistler had the audacity to send for the great throat specialist Mackenzie.

Sir Morell, when he saw that he had been called in to treat a dog, didn't like it much, it was plain. But he said nothing. He prescribed, pocketed a big fee, and drove away.

The next day he sent post-haste for Whistler; and Whistler, thinking he was summoned on some matter connected with his beloved dog, dropped his work and rushed like the wind to Mackenzie's.

On his arrival Sir Morell said gravely:

"How do you do, Mr. Whistler? I wanted to see you about having my front door painted."

* * * * *

A story is told of a very popular cavalry officer. He was being tried for drunkenness, and among other witnesses was his Irish orderly. The court, anxious to give the officer every chance, put several questions to this witness with a view of eliciting any facts that might be in his master's favor. When the orderly said that his master, on going to bed, had expressed a wish to be called early, the members of the court-martial were distinctly pleased.

A man who gave special instructions to be called early could not, surely—they argued to themselves—have been drunk. Hoping to get favorable particulars, the judge advocate put a further question.

"And why did the major wish to be called early?" he asked.

"Faith, an' he tould me it was because he was to be Queen of the May," came the answer.

That settled it.

* * * * *

A college professor, noted for his concentration of thought, returned home from a scientific meeting one night, still pondering deeply upon the subject that had been discussed. As he entered his room he heard a noise that seemed to come from under the bed.

"Is there some one there?" he asked absently.

"No, professor," answered the intruder, who knew of his peculiarities.

"That's strange," muttered the professor. "I was almost sure I heard some one under the bed."

* * * * *

Fond Mother—"Jane, has Johnny come home from school yet?"

Jane—"I think so. I haven't seen him, but the cat is hiding under the stove."

* * * * *

Somebody told Mr. Jenks that red flannel worn next to the skin would cure the rheumatism from which he suffered. So he purchased several sets of red flannel undergarments. The clerk assured him that the firm guaranteed the goods in every particular. About two months later, says the New York "Times," Mr. Jenks revisited the shop, sought out the proprietor and told his woful story.

"The goods are the best in the house," declared the proprietor. "Of course," he said, in a reasonable tone used on unreasonable persons, "of course the shirts may have shrunk or faded a little—"

"Shrunk! Faded!" bellowed Mr. Jenks. "What do you think my wife said to me, when I came down to breakfast yesterday with one of them on?"

The proprietor looked bored.

"Well, sir," said the aggrieved Jenks, "she looked at me a minute, and then said, 'What is that little red line round your neck John? It isn't the baby's string of coral beads, is it?'"

* * * * *

"Now, Tommy," said Mrs. Bull, "I want you to be good while I'm out."

"I'll be good for a nickel," replied Tommy.

"Tommy," she said, "I want you to remember that you can not be a son of mine unless you are good for nothing."

* * * * *

Bill Jones is a country storekeeper down in Louisiana, and last spring he went to New Orleans to purchase a stock of goods. The goods were shipped immediately and reached home before he did. When the boxes of goods were delivered at his store by the drayman his wife happened to look at the largest; she uttered a loud cry and called for a hammer. A neighbor, hearing the screams, rushed to her assistance and asked what was the matter. The wife, pale and faint, pointed to an inscription on the box which read as follows:

"Bill inside."

* * * * *

Customer—"Are these five or six wedding rings all you have in stock? Why, you've got a whole trayful of engagement rings."

Jeweler—"Yes, sir, and it will take that whole trayful of engagement rings to work off those five or six wedding rings."

* * * * *

They were newly married and on a honeymoon trip. They put up at a sky-scraper hotel. The bridegroom felt indisposed, and the bride said she would slip out and do a little shopping.

In due time she returned and tripped blithely up to her room, a little awed by the number of doors that looked all alike. But she was sure of her own and tapped gently on the panel.

"I'm back, honey; let me in," she whispered.

No answer.

"Honey, honey, let me in!" she called again, rapping louder. Still no answer.

"Honey, honey, it's Mabel. Let me in."

There was silence for several seconds; then a man's voice, cold and full of dignity, came from the other side of the door:

"Madame, this is not a beehive; it's a bathroom."

* * * * *

Leigh Hunt was asked by a lady at dessert if he would not venture on an orange. "Madam," he replied, "I should be happy to do so, but I am afraid I should tumble off."

* * * * *

Mrs. Prattle looked at her visitor with reproach in her wide blue eyes. "Talk," she said eagerly, "our baby talk? Well, I guess he can. He's three months younger than my cousin's boy and he's a year ahead of him in language. You know often people tell you their children can say things, and when you hear them you have to work hard with your imagination to tell what they're saying.

"Now, there's my cousin's baby—the one I spoke of. They declare that child has a vocabulary of fifteen words, but, my dear, if you could hear him. He says 'bay' for bread, and 'flis' for fish, and 'cang' for candle, and 'hort' for horse, and 'apa' for father. Now I'll try Harold with those very words, and you'll see the difference.

"Say bread, Harold—bread—bre-e-ad."

"Wed," said the baby.

"Now say fish, fi-sh."

"Whish," said the baby.

"And now horse," said Harold's mother. "Horse—ho-orse, ho-r-se."

"Woss," said the baby.

"And now will precious say father, fa-ather, fa-a-ar-ther?"

"Wahwah," said the baby.

"There, you see!" cried Mrs. Prattle in triumph. "He seems to catch the sound of every word. Now say good-by, darling, and then nurse will take you upstairs. Good-by—goo-ood-by-y-y."

"Wy wy," said the baby.

* * * * *

The superintendent of a Sunday-school class in Philadelphia recently called upon a visitor to "say a few words" to the class, the members of which are mostly children of tender age.

The visitor, a speaker well known for his verbose and circumlocutory mode of speech, began his address as follows:

"This morning, children, I purpose to offer you an epitome of the life of St. Paul. It may be perhaps that there are among you some too young to grasp the meaning of the word 'epitome.'

"'Epitome,' children, is in its signification synonymous with synopsis."

* * * * *

A milliner endeavored to sell to a colored woman one of the last season's hats at a very moderate price. It was a big white picture-hat.

"Law, no, honey!" exclaimed the woman. "I could nevah wear that. I'd look jes' like a blueberry in a pan of milk."

* * * * *

A few years ago the celebrated Potter family, of which Bishop Potter was a member, held a reunion the chief feature of which was a banquet. During the banquet the various heads of the different families of Potters arose and gave a short account of the pedigrees and deeds of their ancestors and each head seemed to be able to demonstrate that their branch was the oldest and most renowned. After all the speakers had finished, Honorable William M. Evarts, who was present as the legal adviser of the New York branch, was called upon for a speech and responded by saying that he felt there was little left for him to say, but after listening to the ancestry and history of the family he felt he could cast his eyes toward heaven and say, "Oh, Lord! thou art the clay and we are the Potters."

* * * * *

A Massachusetts minister was making his first visit to Kentucky several years ago. He had to spend the night in a small mountain town where feuds and moonshine still abounded. Engaging in conversation with one of the natives, he said:

"My friend, this is a very bibulous State, I hear."

"Lord!" replied the man, "there hain't twenty-five Bibles in all Kentucky."

* * * * *

An elderly gentleman opposed to the use of tobacco approached a young man who stood on a street corner smoking a cigar, and asked him severely, "How many cigars a day do you smoke?" "Three," was the reply. "How much do you pay for them?" he went on. "Fifteen cents each," replied the young man patiently. "Do you realize," went on his inquisitor, "that if you would save that money, by the time you are as old as I am you would own that big building on the corner?" "Do *you* own it?" inquired the smoker. "No," was the response. "Well, I do," said the young man.

* * * * *

EVERYBODY'S FRIEND IN NOVA SCOTIA

J. R. FULLER,

Dealer in
Soft and Hard Coal, Ice Cream,
Wood, Lime, Cement, Perfumery, Nails,
Putty, Spectacles, and Horse Radish.
Chocolate Caramels and Tar Roofing,
Gas-Fitting and Undertaking in all
its Branches.

Hides, Tallow, and Maple Sirup, Fine Gold
Jewelry, Silverware, and Salt, Glue,
Codfish, and Gents' Neckwear.
Undertaker and Confectioner.
Diseases of Horses and Children a
Specialty.

Five Islands, N. S.

* * * * *

A Lady going out for the day locked everything up carefully, and for the grocer's benefit left a card on the back door.

"All out. Don't leave anything," it read.

On her return she found her house ransacked and all her choicest possessions gone. To the card on the door was added, "Thanks. We haven't left much."

* * * * *

"Edward Everett Hale," said a lawyer, "was one of the guests at a millionaire's dinner.

"The millionaire was a free spender, but he wanted full credit for every dollar put out.

"And as the dinner progressed, he told his guests what the more expensive dishes had cost.

"'This terrapin,' he would say, 'was shipped direct from Baltimore. A Baltimore cook came on to prepare it. The dish actually cost one dollar a teaspoonful.'

"So he talked of the fresh peas, the hot-house asparagus, the Covent Garden peaches, and the other courses. He dwelt especially on the expense of the large and beautiful grapes, each bunch a foot long, each grape bigger than a plum. He told down to a penny what he had figured it out that the grapes had cost him apiece.

"The guests looked annoyed. They ate the expensive grapes charily. But Dr. Hale, smiling, extended his plate and said:

"'Would you mind cutting me off about $1.87 worth more, please?'"

* * * * *

Joe Jefferson had but one person with him who did not reverence the man and the name.

This individual, one Bagley by name, was the property man and annoyed the great comedian with undue familiarity. He had called Mr. Jefferson "Joey" during his entire thirty years' service.

Just previous to an auspicious opening in one of the big cities, Mr. Jefferson discharged Bagley for humiliating him before a number of friends. Bagley got drunk right away, and that night paid his way to the gallery to see Mr. Jefferson present "Rip Van Winkle." The angry Frau has just driven poor, destitute Rip from the cottage when Rip turns and, with a world of pathos, asks: "Den haf I no interest in dis house?" The house is deathly still, the audience half in tears, when Bagley's cracked voice responds: "Only eighty per cent, Joey—only eighty per cent."

* * * * *

Dean Hole, the noted English clergyman who died recently, was the leading figure in many humorous stories. On one occasion he was crossing the Channel after a visit to the Continent, the voyage being very stormy.

The Dean was a bad sailor and had suffered a great deal on the trip. At Dover he was looking over the railway company's rules on the station wall as a passenger came up. Said the Dean: "After that stormy voyage we have at least one advantage in making the subsequent trip to London. I see the company carries returning empties at reduced rates."

* * * * *

Gilbert Stuart, though a celebrated artist, was likewise a great braggart. On one occasion a great public dinner was given to Isaac Hull by the town of Boston, and he was asked to sit for his picture to the artist.

When Hull visited the studio Stuart took great delight in entertaining him with anecdotes of his English success, stories of the marquis of this and the baroness of that, which showed how elegant was the society to which he had been accustomed.

Unfortunately, in the midst of this grandeur, Mrs. Stuart, who did not know that there was a sitter, came in with apron on and her head tied up with some handkerchiefs, from the kitchen, and cried out: "Do you mean to have that leg of mutton boiled or roasted?" to which Stuart replied, with great presence of mind, "Ask your mistress."

* * * * *

This story is related of an old-time Judge in Sullivan County, N. Y.:

During a session of court there was so much talking and laughter going on that the Judge, becoming angry and confused, shouted in great wrath:

"Silence, here! We have decided half a dozen cases this morning, and I have not heard a word of one of them."

* * * * *

Irving Bacheller, the author of "Eben Holden," went a little farther north than usual one summer while on his vacation, and penetrated Newfoundland. He caught a good many fish, but this did not prevent his keeping an eye on the natives. He was particularly impressed by the men who spent the day lounging about the village stores.

"What do you fellows do when you sit around the store like this?" he asked of the crowd arranged in a circle of tilted chairs and empty boxes and maintaining a profound silence.

"Well," drawled one of the oldest, "sometimes we set and think, and then again other times we jest set."

* * * * *

Not long before his death Thomas B. Reed visited some friends at their summer residence at Watch Hill, R. I. Late in the afternoon he was driven up to Westerly to take the 7 o'clock train for Boston. It was a warm evening, the horses lagged and he missed the train, the last Boston-bound train stopping at Westerly that night.

As Mr. Reed had an important engagement in Boston early the next day, he seemed worried until he learned that there was a Boston express which passed Westerly at 9 o'clock. Then he smiled.

Going to the telegraph office, he directed a telegram to the superintendent of the road in Boston, and sent the following message:

"Will you stop the 9 o'clock express at Westerly to-night for a large party for Boston."

The answer came: "Yes. Will stop train."

Mr. Reed read the message, and smiled. When the train pulled in Mr. Reed quietly started to board it, when the conductor said: "Where is that large party we were to stop for?"

"I am the large party," replied Mr. Reed, and he boarded the train.

* * * * *

Wilfred was sitting upon his father's knee watching his mother arranging her hair.

"Papa hasn't any Marcel waves like that," said the father, laughingly.

Wilfred, looking up at his father's bald pate, replied, "Nope; no waves; it's all beach."

* * * * *

The Prince of Wales is fond of telling a good story to his friends in connection with his visit to Ottawa some few years ago. The Prince—then Duke of York—stole away for a quiet bicycle spin early one morning, and in his ramblings met a farmer, heading marketward, his wagon temporarily stalled by the loss of a nut belonging to the whiffletree bolt. His Royal Highness, with his usual democratic kindness, assisted him in putting things right. On parting, the farmer expressed his rough thanks and asked if he might know the name of the person to whom he was indebted. The royal cyclist replied modestly: "I am the Duke of York. And may I ask whom I have the pleasure of addressing?" A broad, amused smile beamed from the farmer's face as he said: "Me! Me! Why, I'm your uncle, the Czar of Russia!"

* * * * *

"All right on behind there?" called the conductor from the front of the car.

"Hold on," cried a shrill voice. "Wait till I get my clothes on!"

The passengers craned their necks expectantly. A small boy was struggling to get a basket of laundry aboard.

* * * * *

One of the jokes of which Kentuckians never grow weary concerns Senator Blackburn and his loyal appreciation of the liquid products of his native State. The Senator had gone to pay a visit to a friend of his who lived many miles distant. His friend met the Senator as he alighted at the station.

"How are you Joe?" his friend asked.

"I'm up against it," was the reply. "I lost the best part of my baggage en route."

"Did you misplace it, or was it stolen?" his friend inquired solicitously.

"Neither," said the Senator. "The cork came out."

* * * * *

Kentucky Tailor—"What size shall I make your hip pockets, Colonel, pint or quart?"

* * * * *

Once, during his second term, Grover Cleveland was asked to speak at a function in a certain town, and when he arrived at the depot the wind was blowing a gale, sleet was driving, and hailstones nearly as large as marbles were fiercely falling. Of course, the inevitable brass band was there, and at the sight of the President the performers struck up with all the strenuosity at their command.

"That is the most realistic music I ever heard," remarked Cleveland.

"What are they trying to play?" asked Secretary Olney, who accompanied him.

"'Hail to the Chief'!" replied the President, with a cheerful smile.

* * * * *

The chaplain of one of his Majesty's ships was giving a magic-lantern lecture, the subject of which was "Scenes from the Bible." He arranged with a sailor who possessed a gramophone to discourse appropriate music between the slides. The first picture shown was Adam and Eve in the Garden of Eden. The sailor cudgeled his brain but could think of nothing suitable. "Play up," whispered the chaplain. Suddenly a large idea struck the jolly tar and to the great consternation of the chaplain and the delight of the audience the gramophone burst forth with the strains of "There's only one girl in the world for me."

* * * * *

The craze for giving and accepting coupons for purchases of merchandise, to be redeemed by prizes, was given a more or less merited rebuke by Nat C. Goodwin. He bought a bill of goods, and the salesman offered him the coupons that the amount of the purchase called for. Mr. Goodwin shook his head. "I don't want 'em," he said.

"You had better take them, sir," persisted the clerk; "we redeem them with very handsome prizes. If you can save up a thousand coupons we give a grand piano."

"Say, look here," replied Mr. Goodwin, "if I ever drank enough of your whisky or smoked enough of your cigars to get a thousand of those coupons I wouldn't want a piano. I'd want a harp."

* * * * *

He—"You've got to have a pull to get ahead."

She—"Yes, and you've got to have a head to get a pull."

* * * * *

A Southern lawyer tells of a case that came to him at the outset of his career, wherein his principal witness was a darky named Jackson, supposed to have knowledge of certain transactions not at all to the credit of his employer, the defendant.

"Now, Jackson," said the lawyer, "I want you to understand the importance of telling the truth when you are put on the stand. You know what will happen, don't you, if you don't tell the truth?"

"Yassir," was Jackson's reply; "in dat case I expects our side will win de case."

* * * * *

The Suitor—"They say that Love is blind."

The Heiress—"But nowadays he has a marvelous sense of touch."

* * * * *

A small boy who had recently passed his fifth birthday was riding in a suburban car with his mother, when they were asked the customary question, "How old is the boy?" After being told the correct age, which did not require a fare, the conductor passed on to the next person.

The boy sat quite still as if pondering over some question, and then, concluding that full information had not been given, called loudly to the conductor, then at the other end of the car: "And mother's thirty-one!"

* * * * *

One of the uptown banks, on a conspicuous corner, gained a bad name with the daily crowd of New York pedestrians. Its financial standing was of course beyond question, but its clock ran on a very eccentric and confusing system. The timepiece stood in a spot easily observable and was consulted for years in spite of its tendency to wander from strict accuracy. A woman excusing her lateness for luncheon said she thought she was on time by the clock in the bank.

"Oh, nobody can go by that," said her companion contemptuously. "We call that the bank where the wild time grows."

* * * * *

In a certain home where the stork recently visited there is a six-year-old son of inquiring mind. When he was first taken in to see the new arrival he exclaimed: "Oh, mamma, it hasn't any teeth! And no hair!" Then, clasping his hands in despair, he cried: "Somebody has done us! It's an old baby."

* * * * *

A prominent railroad man hurried down the lobby of a Binghamton hotel and up to the desk. He had just ten minutes in which to pay his bill and reach the station. Suddenly it occurred to him that he had forgotten something.

"Here, boy," he called to a negro bellboy, "run up to 48 and see if I left a box on the bureau. And be quick about it, will you?"

The boy rushed up the stairs. The ten minutes dwindled to seven and the railroad man paced the office. At length the boy appeared.

"Yas, suh," he panted breathlessly. "Yas, suh, yo' left it, suh!"

* * * * *

A Boston minister tells of a little girl friend of his who, one day, proudly displayed for his admiration a candy cat.

"Are you going to eat it?" the minister asked.

"No, sir; it's too pretty to eat. I'm going to keep it," the little girl replied, as she stroked it with a moist little hand.

Several days later the minister saw her again, and inquired about the cat.

A regretful look came into her eyes.

"It's gone," she sighed. "You see, I saved it and saved it, till it got so dirty that I just *had* to eat it."

* * * * *

"Only fools are certain, Tommy; wise men hesitate."

"Are you sure, uncle?"

"Yes, my boy; certain of it."

* * * * *

"My rubber," said Nat Goodwin, describing a Turkish bath that he once had in Mexico, "was a very strong man. He laid me on a slab and kneaded me and punched me and banged me in a most emphatic way. When it was over and I had gotten up, he came up behind me before my sheet was adjusted, and gave me three resounding slaps on the bare back with the palm of his enormous hand.

"'What in blazes are you doing?' I gasped, staggering.

"'No offense, sir,' said the man. 'It was only to let the office know that I was ready for the next bather. You see, sir, the bell's out of order in this room.'"

* * * * *

"I want to know," said the irate matron, "how much money my husband drew out of this bank last week." "I can't give you that information, ma'am," answered the man in the cage. "You're the paying teller, aren't you?" "Yes, but I'm not the telling payer."

* * * * *

A lady once showed her little girl a beautiful new silk dress which had just arrived from the dressmaker, and by way of improving the occasion she said: "You know, dear, all this was given us by a poor worm." The little girl looked puzzled for a minute or two and then said: "Do you mean dad, mama?"

* * * * *

When Blaine was a young lawyer, and cases were few, he was asked to defend a poverty-stricken tramp accused of stealing a watch. He pleaded with all the ardor at his command, drawing so pathetic a picture with such convincing energy that at the close of his argument the court was in tears and even the tramp wept. The jury deliberated but a few minutes and returned the verdict "not guilty." Then the tramp drew himself up, tears streaming down his face as he looked at the future "Plumed Knight," and said: "Sir, I have never heard so grand a plea, I have not cried before since I was a child. I have no money with which to reward you, but (drawing a package from the depths of his ragged clothes), here's that watch; take it and welcome."

* * * * *

The other day an ingenious-looking person called with the message to the housewife that her husband had sent him for his dress suit, which was to be pressed and redone by the tailor.

"Dear me," said the housewife, "he said nothing to me about it. Did he look quite well?"

"Yes, mum; he wuz in good health and spirits."

"And he seemed quite as if he knew what he was about?"

"He did that, mum."

"And did he look as if he were quite content with things about him?"

"He was all that, mum."

"Well," said the lady, "it seems strange that he should only think of that dress suit now, because it's ten years since he's dead and buried, and I've often wondered how he's been getting on."

* * * * *

Two friends were walking down Bond Street, London. A man came up and saluted the elder: "How do you do, Lord — —?"

"Ah! how-do? Glad to see you. How's the old complaint?"

The stranger's face clouded over and he shook his head. "No better."

"Dear me; so sorry. Glad to have met you. Good-by."

"Who's your friend?" asked the other, when the stranger was gone.

"No idea."

"Why, you asked him about his old complaint!"

"Pooh, pooh!" replied the nobleman, unconcernedly. "The old fellow's well over sixty; bound to have something the matter with him."

* * * * *

"Did you tip the waiter?"

"Yes, so to speak. I turned him down."

* * * * *

Dr. Jowett of Oxford was a formidable wit. At a gathering at which he was present the talk ran upon the comparative gifts of two Balliol men who had been made respectively a judge and a bishop. Prof. Henry Smith, famous in his day for his brilliancy, pronounced the bishop to be the greater man of the two for this reason: "A judge, at the most, can only say, 'You be hanged,' whereas a bishop can say, 'You be damned!'"

"Yes," said Dr. Jowett, but if the judge says, "'You be hanged,' you *are* hanged."

* * * * *

"I'm so glad you've come. We're going to have a young married couple for dinner."

"I'm glad too. They ought to be tender."

* * * * *

"I pay as I go," declared the pompous citizen.

"Not while I'm running these apartments," declared the janitor. "You'll pay as you move in."

* * * * *

Among seven distinguished men who were to speak at the opening exercises of a new school was a professor well known for his lapses of memory. But his speech was clear that night, and as he seated himself his loving wife felt that he had fully earned the burst of applause that followed, and she clapped her little hands enthusiastically. Then her cheeks crimsoned.

"Did you see anything amusing about the close of my address, my dear?" asked the Professor as they started for home. "It seemed as if I heard sounds suggestive of merriment about me."

"Well, dear," said she, "of all the people who applauded your address, you clapped the loudest and longest."

* * * * *

Teacher—"What is the Hague tribunal?"

Willie—"The Hague tribunal ar—"

Teacher—"Don't say 'The Hague tribunal are,' Willie; use is."

Willie—"The Hague tribunal isbitrates national controversies."

* * * * *

Sir Wilfrid Laurier was once on an electioneering tour in Ontario and, as the elections were bitterly contested, every effort was made to stir up race and religious prejudice. One day a Quebec Liberal sent this telegram to Sir Wilfrid: "Report in circulation in this country that your children have not been baptized. Telegraph denial." To this the Premier replied: "Sorry to say report is correct. I have no children."

* * * * *

The teacher of one of the rooms in a school in the suburbs of Cleveland had been training her pupils in anticipation of a visit from the school commissioner. At last he came, and the classes were called out to show their attainments.

The arithmetic class was the first called, and in order to make a good impression the teacher put the first question to Johnny Smith, the star pupil.

"Johnny, if coal is selling at $6 per ton, and you pay the coal dealer $24, how many tons of coal will he bring you?"

"Three," was the prompt reply from Johnny.

The teacher, much embarrassed, said, "Why, Johnny, that isn't right."

"Oh, I know it ain't, but they do it anyhow."

* * * * *

A publisher who occupied a loft in New York directed one of his clerks to hang out a "Boy wanted" sign at the entrance. The card had been swaying in the breeze only a few minutes when a red-headed little tad climbed to the publisher's office with the sign under his arm.

"Say, mister," he demanded of the publisher, "did youse hang out this here 'Boy Wanted' sign?"

"I did," replied the publisher sternly. "Why did you tear it down?"

"Hully gee!" he blurted. "Why, I'm the boy!" And he was.

* * * * *

A distinguished surgeon, Dr. Abernethy by name, famed for his laconic speech as well as for his professional skill, met one day his equal in a woman of few words, who came to him with a hand badly swollen and inflamed.

"Burn?" asked the doctor.

"Bruise."

"Poultice."

The next day the patient returned and the dialogue was resumed.

"Better?"

"Worse."

"More poultice."

Two days later the woman called again, and this was the conversation:

"Better?"

"Well. Fee?"

"Nothing!" exclaimed the doctor. "Most sensible woman I ever met!"

* * * * *

Visitor—"Well, Harold, what are you going to be when you grow up?"

Harold—"Oh, I'm going to be a sailor; but baby's only going to be just an ordinary father."

** * * * **

No amount of persuasion or punishment could keep Johnnie from running away. The excitement of being pursued and of being brought back to a tearful family appealed to his sense of the dramatic and offset the slight discomfort that sometimes followed.

Finally his mother determined upon a new method. She decided, after many misgivings, that the next time Johnnie ran away no notice whatever should be taken of it. He should stay away as long as he pleased and return when he saw fit.

In a few days the youngster again disappeared. His mother was firm in her resolve and no search was made. Great was poor Johnnie's disappointment. He managed to stay away all day, but when it began to grow dark his courage failed and he started for home. He sneaked ignominiously into the kitchen. Nobody spoke to him. Apparently his absence had not been noticed. This was too much. As soon as opportunity offered he remarked casually, "Well, I see you've got the same old cat."

** * * * **

A gentleman who happened to come in rather late at a dinner found that the guests had finished soup and were on with the next course. When he had sat down a waiter came up and said, "Soup, sir?" "No, thanks," he replied, whereupon the waiter went away. Another waiter, seeing he had nothing, said to him, "Soup, sir?" He replied rather testily, "No, thank you." A third waiter, who saw him come in and took compassion on him, placed the soup in front of him. "Look here, my man, is this compulsory?" "No, sir; it's mulligatawny," replied the waiter.

** * * * **

A big, burly, fierce-looking man and a meek, inoffensive-looking little chap were sawing timber with a cross-cut saw. A strapping Irishman, passing that way, stopped to watch them. Back and forth, back and forth, they pulled at the saw. Finally the Irishman could stand it no longer. With a whoop and a yell he rushed at the big man and brought him to the ground, burying his knees deep into the sawyer's chest.

Biff! Bang! Thump! Biff!

"There," he said, letting him have one parting blow square on the nose, "now m'bbe ye'll let the little felly hev it!"

** * * * **

Oliver Herford once entered a doubtful-looking restaurant in a small New York town and ordered a lamb-chop. After a long delay the waiter returned, bearing a plate on which reposed a dab of mashed potatoes and a much overdone chop of microscopical proportions with a remarkably long and slender rib attached. This the waiter set down before him and then hurried away.

"See here," called Herford, "I ordered a chop."

"Yessir," replied the man, "there it is."

"Ah, so it is," replied Herford, peering at it closely. "I thought it was a crack in the plate."

* * * * *

In one of the elevators of a city skyscraper, as the elevator shot toward the zenith, a stout man began to sputter. "Bub-but, rt-st-st-b'r'r'r," he said, as the veins stood out upon his neck. At the twenty-third story the stout man's eyes were nearly starting from his head, and as he grasped the arm of the elevator man the latter nervously pulled the lever, and the lift started for the bottom at a terrific rate. The solitary passenger danced about, gurgling spasmodically. As the car struck bottom, however, he rushed through the door and up to an important individual, whose cap bore the screed "Starter." "S-s-s-say," he sputtered, "t-t-this is the th-th-third trip I-I-I've t-t-taken in the elevator, 'n' I-I-I-I w-w-wanter g-g-g-get off at the sev-sev-seventh fl-fl-fl-floor. Before I-I-I c-c-c-can say sev-sev-seven I-I-I-I'm up to the t-t-top, 'n' be-be-before I-I-I can cat-cat-catch my br-br-breath I-I-I'm down h-h-here again, 'n' I-I-I-I'm in a de-de-vil of a hurry."

* * * * *

Nervous player (deprecatingly playing card)—"I really don't know what to play. I'm afraid I've made a fool of myself."

Partner (reassuringly)—"That all right. I don't see what else you could have done!"

* * * * *

Some of Darwin's boy friends once plotted a surprise for the naturalist. They slew a centipede, glued on it a beetle's head, and also added to its body the wings of a butterfly and the long legs of a grasshopper. Then they put the new insect in a box and knocked at the great man's door. "We found this in the fields," they cried with eager voices. "Do tell us what it can be." Darwin looked at the strange compound and then at the boys' innocent faces. "Did it hum when you caught it?" he asked. "Oh yes, sir," they answered quickly, nudging one another, "it hummed like anything." "Then," said the philosopher, "it is a humbug."

* * * * *

A man had been sent by the house-agents to take an inventory of the drawing-room furniture. He was so long about his task that at last the mistress of the house went to see what was taking place. She found the man slumbering sweetly on the sofa with an empty bottle beside him; it was evident, however, that he had made a pathetic though solitary attempt to do his work, for in the inventory book was written, "One revolving carpet."

* * * * *

The customs of military service require officers to visit the kitchens during cooking hours to see that the soldiers' food is properly prepared. One old colonel, who let it be pretty generally known that his orders must be obeyed without question or explanation, once stopped two soldiers who were carrying a soup-kettle out of a kitchen.

"Here, you," he growled, "give me a taste of that."

One of the soldiers ran and fetched a ladle and gave the colonel the desired taste. The colonel spat and spluttered.

"Good heavens, man! You don't call that stuff soup, do you?"

"No, sir," replied the soldier meekly, "it's dishwater we was emptyin', sir."

* * * * *

The ship upon clearing the harbor ran into a half-pitching, half-rolling sea, that became particularly noticeable about the time the twenty-five passengers at the captain's table sat down to dinner.

"I hope that all twenty-five of you will have a pleasant trip," the captain told them as the soup appeared, "and that this little assemblage of twenty-four will reach port much benefited by the voyage. I look upon these twenty-two smiling faces much as a father does upon his family, for I am responsible for the safety of this group of seventeen. I hope that all thirteen of you will join me later in drinking to a merry trip. I believe that we seven fellow passengers are most congenial and I applaud the judgment which chose from the passenger list these three persons for my table. You and I, my dear, sir, are—Here, steward! Bring on the fish and clear away these dishes."

* * * * *

"Extra Billy" Smith, the Confederate General, was one of the most irascible as well as one of the most patriotic of men. Upon one occasion he was leading a regiment on a long and difficult march. Weary and exhausted they halted for a rest by the wayside. When it became necessary to move on, the General gave the order, but the tired men remained stretched upon the ground. The order was repeated peremptorily. Still no motion. By this time the temper of the General was at white heat. He thundered out:

"If you don't get up and start at once I'll march the regiment off and leave every d——d one of you behind."

They started.

* * * * *

A Boston lawyer, who brought his wit from his native Dublin, while cross-examining the plaintiff in a divorce trial, brought forth the following:

"You wish to divorce this woman because she drinks?"

"Yes, sir."

"Do you drink yourself?"

"That's *my* business!"—angrily.

Whereupon the unmoved lawyer asked:

"Have you any other business?"

* * * * *

One rainy afternoon Aunt Sue was explaining the meaning of various words to her young nephew. "Now, an heirloom, my dear, means something that has been handed down from father to son," she said.

"Well," replied the boy thoughtfully, "that's a queer name for my pants."

* * * * *

"The easiest money that I ever made," said a shipping man the other day, "was handed to me in New York not long ago. I was visiting there and had a little time to myself, so I bought a paper and went down to the river front. I saw an advertisement in the paper saying that a tug was to be auctioned off that day, so I went to the place and stood around examining the tug. After a while a man who had been watching me came over and began asking questions. I told him I was interested in boats and was from Philadelphia. Then he asked: 'What are you doing down here?' 'I came down to this auction sale,' I said. 'Well,' said the man, 'if you want to keep on the right side of the boys you'll do something for me. Here's $100; do not bid on the tug.' I took the money and departed. I had not the slightest intention of bidding."

* * * * *

A bride and groom had been much troubled by the stares of people at hotels wherever they went. So when they arrived at the next hotel the groom called the colored head-waiter.

"Now, George," he said, "we have been bothered to death by people staring at us because we are just married. We want to be free from that sort of thing here. Now, here's two dollars, and remember I trust you not to tell people that we are just married, if they ask you. Understand?"

"Yas, sah!" said George; "I un'stand."

All went well that day. But the following morning when the couple came down to breakfast the staring was worse than ever. Chambermaids in the hall snickered; the clerks behind the desk nudged each other; everybody in the dining-room stared. When the couple returned to their room it was only to see a head sticking out of nearly every room down the long hall.

This was too much.

This *was* the limit!

Angered beyond control, the groom went to the desk and called for the head-waiter.

"Look here, you old fool," said the groom, "didn't I give you two dollars to protect my wife and myself from the staring business?"

"Yas, sah, you did," said George. "'Pon me soul, I didn't tell, sah."

"Then how about this staring?" asked the irate groom. "It's worse here than anywhere. Did anybody ask if we were married?"

"Yas, sah; several folks did," replied George.

"Well, what did you tell them?"

"I tole 'em, sah," replied the honest negro, "you wuzn't married at all."

* * * * *

A witty priest was once visiting a "self-made" millionaire, who took him to see his seldom-used library.

"There," said the millionaire, pointing to a table covered with books, "there are my best friends."

"Ah," replied the wit, as he glanced at the leaves, "I'm glad you don't cut them!"

* * * * *

Mrs. Maloney was before the Judge, charged with assault on Policeman Casey. She had been unusually attentive throughout the proceedings, and now the Judge was summing up the evidence.

"The evidence shows, Mrs. Maloney," he began, "that you threw a stone at Policeman Casey."

"It shows more than that, yer Honor," interrupted Mrs. Maloney; "it shows that Oi hit him."

* * * * *

When Mark Twain was a young and struggling newspaper writer, in San Francisco, a lady of his acquaintance saw him one day with a cigar-box under his arm looking in a shop window.

"Mr. Clemens," she said, "I always see you with a cigar-box under your arm. I am afraid you are smoking too much."

"It isn't that," said Mark. "I'm moving again."

* * * * *

A thunderstorm overtook the Emperor Francis Joseph of Austria when out shooting in 1873 with old Emperor William of Germany and Victor Emmanuel. The three monarchs got separated from their party and lost their way. They were drenched to the skin, and, in search of shelter, hailed a peasant driving a covered cart drawn by oxen along the high road. The peasant took up the royal trio and drove on.

"And who may you be, for you are a stranger in these parts?" he asked, after a while, of Emperor William.

"I am the Emperor of Germany," replied his Teutonic majesty.

"Ha, very good," said the peasant, and then, addressing Victor Emmanuel, "and you, my friend?"

"Why, I am the King of Italy," came the prompt reply.

"Ha, ha, very good, indeed! And who are you?" addressing Francis Joseph.

"I am the Emperor of Austria," said the latter.

The peasant then scratched his head and said with a knowing wink: "Very good, and who do you suppose I am?"

Their majesties replied they would like very much to know.

"Why, I am his Holiness the Pope."

* * * * *

In a cemetery at Middlebury, Vt., is a stone, erected by a widow to her loving husband, bearing this inscription:

"Rest in peace—until we meet again."

* * * * *

Mrs. Gilroy, prominent in the church work of her small city, had acquired a new servant, willing but ignorant.

"Bridget," she said, "I am going to lie down and do not wish to be disturbed. If any one calls, do not say I am not at home, but give an evasive answer."

"What's that, mum?" said Bridget.

Having explained as well as she could, the good lady retired and later appeared below stairs, much refreshed.

"Did any one call?" she asked.

"Yes, mum; the new minister, from your church."

"Oh, Bridget. What did you tell him?"

"Well," sez he, "is Mrs. Gilroy at home?" and I sez nuthin', and sez he a little louder, "Is Mrs. Gilroy at home?" and sez I, "Was your grandmother a monkey?"

* * * * *

A young kindergarten teacher, of Manhattan, who is made much of by her pupils—frequently meeting their parents—has a very affable manner, and, on entering a Broadway car recently, exclaimed in her most cordial way to one of the passengers: "Why, how do you do, Mr. Brown!" As the man addressed evidently did not know her and looked rather dazed, she saw her mistake and hurriedly apologized, saying: "Oh, I beg your pardon-I thought you were the father of one of my children."

Then every one within hearing looked so amused that the young lady left the car at the next stop.

* * * * *

A Mr. Johnson, of Boston, was the owner of a small yacht, in which he took much pleasure during the summer, cruising along the coast.

He had for a cook a young fellow from Denmark whose English was not always perfect, but who made himself so generally useful that Mr. Johnson kept him for several years at good wages. One summer they landed at a place where a camp-meeting was in full blast. Our friend, the Dane, was greatly interested and took a front seat.

Near the close of the meeting one of the brethren went about among the people exhorting them to "go forward." Coming to the Dane, he said, "My friend, don't you want to work for Jesus?"

"No," said the Dane, "I've got a good yob with Yohnson."

* * * * *

Johnny—"Pa, did Moses have the dyspepsia like you?"

Father—"How on earth do I know? What makes you ask such a question?"

"Why, our Sunday-school teacher says the Lord gave Moses two tablets."

* * * * *

Elderly Aunt—"I suppose you wondered, dear little Hans, why I left you so abruptly in the lane. I saw a man, and oh, how I ran!"

Hans—"Did you get him?"

* * * * *

A man returned home late one night after having partaken rather freely of the "cup that cheers." All might have been well had not one tree intercepted between him and his destination—one solitary tree at the foot of his own steps; but Mr. B—— suddenly came into such forcible contact with that tree that he was almost stunned. After recovering his senses, he wandered about, but repeatedly bumped into the same inoffensive barrier. At length he sank down on the ground and muttered helplessly:

"Lost! Lost! in an impenetrable forest!"

* * * * *

The intoxicated individual who, after bumping into the same tree thirteen times, bemoaned the fact that he was lost in an impenetrable forest, is no greater disgrace to modern civilization than the hero of this story:

A citizen of Seattle who had looked upon the wine when he was no longer sure what color it was, in the course of his journey home encountered a tree protected by an iron tree-guard. Grasping the bars, he cautiously felt his way around it twice.

"Curse it!" he moaned, sinking to the ground in despair. "Locked in!"

* * * * *

Stanley, aged four, was one of a large family. Besides numerous sisters and brothers, there were aunts and uncles galore and many cousins. The only very young people, however, were those in his immediate household.

One Thanksgiving dinner Stanley gazed solemnly around the table for a while, and then announced, oracularly:

"My mother and the cat seem to be the only people in this whole family that have any children!"

* * * * *

A clergyman was being shaved by a barber, who had evidently become unnerved by the previous night's dissipation. Finally he cut the clergyman's chin. The latter looked up at the artist reproachfully, and said:

"You see, my man, what comes of hard drinking."

"Yes, sir," replied the barber consolingly, "it makes the skin tender."

* * * * *

Mistress—"Did the mustard plaster do you any good, Bridget?"

Maid—"Yes; but, begorry, mum, ut do bite the tongue!"

* * * * *

They had just met; conversation was somewhat fitful. Finally he decided to guide it into literary channels, where he was more at home, and, turning to his companion, asked:

"Are you fond of literature?"

"Passionately," she replied. "I love books dearly."

"Then you must admire Sir Walter Scott," he exclaimed with sudden animation. "Is not his 'Lady of the Lake' exquisite in its flowing grace and poetic imagery? Is it not—"

"It is perfectly lovely," she assented, clasping her hands in ecstasy. "I suppose I have read it a dozen times."

"And Scott's 'Marmion,'" he continued, "with its rugged simplicity and marvelous description—one can almost smell the heather on the heath while perusing its splendid pages."

"It is perfectly grand," she murmured.

"And Scott's 'Peveril of the Peak' and his noble 'Bride of Lammermoor'—where in the English language will you find anything more heroic than his grand auld Scottish characters and his graphic, forceful pictures of feudal times and customs? You like them, I am sure."

"I just dote upon them," she replied.

"And Scott's Emulsion," he continued hastily, for a faint suspicion was beginning to dawn upon him.

"I think," she interrupted rashly, "that it's the best thing he ever wrote."

* * * * *

"Why is Jones growing a beard?"

"Oh, I believe his wife made him a present of some ties."

* * * * *

Wife—"Do come over to Mrs. Barker's with me, John. She'll make you feel just as if you were at home."

Her Husband — "Then what's the use of going?"

* * * * *

About forty years ago, walking down Market street, in this city, I heard a darky commenting on a sign he had just spelt out, stretched across the sidewalk in front of a livery stable:

"Jist like 'em. Aftah dars no moh slabry dey stick up signs foh me: 'Man-ure Free'!"

* * * * *

In the audience at a lecture on China there was a very pious old lady who was slightly deaf. She thought the lecturer was preaching, and every time he came to a period she would say "Amen!" or some other pious exclamation. The people in the audience, which was composed mostly of the village church members, knew she was being reverent and did not even smile when she exclaimed, until finally the lecturer mentioned some far-off city in China, saying, "I live there." At this point clearly and distinctly could be heard the old lady, saying, "Thank God for that."

* * * * *

A pushing young actor who was playing understudy in one of Mr. Barrie's plays found his opportunity one night through the illness of his principal. He accordingly flooded his managerial and influential acquaintances with telegrams announcing: "I play So-and-So's part to-night." Except that the theater was comparatively empty this breathless disclosure produced no result, except a telegram in reply from Mr. Barrie, to this effect: "Thanks for the warning."

* * * * *

It was a busy day in the butcher-shop. The butcher yelled to the boy who helped him out in the shop: "Hurry up, John, and don't forget to cut off Mrs. Murphy's leg, and break Mrs. Jones's bones, and don't forget to slice Mrs. Johnson's tongue."

* * * * *

Ralph Waldo Emerson, like other men of genius, was absent-minded, and, when a fit of inspiration seized him, he was oblivious to the things of earth to a ludicrous extent. A story that is vouched for as true illustrates this.

The old-fashioned matches, in use in New England in Emerson's time, were made in cards, or flat slabs, the matches being joined at the foot, and separating at the top, like the teeth of a deep comb. Emerson was accustomed, in the midnight watches, to lie awake communing with his own thoughts, and, if any especial inspiration developed itself, he would get up and write it down, lighting the lamp for that purpose.

One night, Mrs. Emerson was awakened by her gifted husband's voice, as he called to her plaintively:

"What is the matter with the matches, my dear? I have struck seven, and not one will light. Where can I get some good ones?"

Mrs. Emerson got out of bed at once, and found the matches in their accustomed place. Her husband had not touched them.

"Why, what can you have been striking, in mistake for matches?" she asked, anxiously, and beheld her best carved tortoise-shell comb, which the absorbed philosopher, had broken up, tooth by tooth, in mistake for the card of matches.

* * * * *

Instructor in Public Speaking—"What is the matter with you, Mr. Jones; can't you speak any louder? Be more enthusiastic. Open your mouth and throw yourself into it."

* * * * *

"I confess that the subject of psychical research makes no great appeal to me," Sir William Henry Perkin, the inventor of coal-tar dyes, told some friends in New York. "Personally, in the course of a fairly long career, I have heard at first hand but one ghost story. Its hero was a man whom I may as well call Snooks.

"Snooks, visiting at a country house, was put in the haunted chamber for the night. He said that he did not feel the slightest uneasiness, but nevertheless, just as a matter of precaution, he took to bed with him a revolver of the latest American pattern.

"He slept peacefully enough until the clock struck two, when he awoke with an unpleasant feeling of oppression. He raised his head and peered about him. The room was wanly illumined by the full moon, and in that weird, bluish light he thought he discerned a small, white hand clasping the rail at the foot of the bed.

"'Who's there?' he asked tremulously.

"There was no reply. The small, white hand did not move.

"'Who's there?' he repeated. 'Answer me or I'll shoot.'

"Again there was no reply.

"Snooks cautiously raised himself, took careful aim and fired.

"From that night on he's limped. Shot off two of his own toes."

* * * * *

When the Rev. Dr. Henson, then of Chicago, came to the New York Chautauqua to lecture on "Fools," Bishop Vincent introduced him thus:

"Ladies and gentlemen, we are now to have a lecture on 'Fools' by one of the most distinguished——"

Here there was a long pause, the Bishop's inflection indicating that he had finished. The audience roared with delight, and roared again, so that it was some time before the sentence was concluded—"men of Chicago."

Dr. Henson, who is a man of ready wit, stepped to the front of the platform, and said:

"Ladies and gentlemen, I am not so great a fool as Bishop Vincent——" and then he paused as if he had finished, and the audience went fairly wild over the situation. When quiet was restored, Dr. Henson concluded—"would have you think."

* * * * *

Doctor (feeling Sandy's pulse in bed)—"What do you drink?"

Sandy (with brightening face)—"Oh, I'm nae particular, doctor! Anything you've got with ye."

* * * * *

Every employee of the Bank of England is required to sign his name in a book on his arrival in the morning, and, if late, must give the reason therefor. The chief cause of tardiness is usually fog, and the first man to arrive writes "fog" opposite his name, and those who follow write "ditto." One day, however, the first late man gave as the reason, "wife had twins," and twenty other late men mechanically signed "ditto" underneath.

* * * * *

At a dinner in Washington there was told a Scotch story of a parishioner who had strayed from his own kirk.

"Why weren't you at the kirk on Sunday?" asked the preacher of the culprit on meeting him a day or two later.

"I was at Mr. McClellan's kirk," said the other.

"I don't like you running about to strange kirks like that," continued the minister. "Not that I object to your hearing Mr. McClellan, but I'm sure you widna like your sheep straying into strange pastures."

"I widna care a grain, sir, if it was better grass," responded the parishioner.

* * * * *

Tommy, very sleepy, was saying his prayers. "Now I lay me down to sleep," he began. "I pray the Lord my soul to keep."

"'If,'" his mother prompted.

"If he hollers let him go, eeny, meeny, miny, mo!"

* * * * *

Perish the thought that the novelist or playwright should be tied down to historical accuracy! Lady Dorothy Neville quotes an amusing correspondence between Bulwer Lytton and her brother, Horace Walpole.

"My dear Walpole: Here I am at Bath—bored to death. I am thinking of writing a play about your great ancestor Sir Robert. Had he not a sister Lucy, and did she not marry a Jacobite?"

Walpole promptly replied:

"My dear Lytton: I care little for my family, and less still for Sir Robert, but I know that he never had a sister Lucy, so she could not have married a Jacobite."

However, this mattered little to Lord Lytton, for his answer ran:

"My dear Walpole: You are too late! Sir Robert *had* a sister Lucy, and she *did* marry a Jacobite."

So in defiance of history, the play "Walpole" was written.

* * * * *

"Here's a curious item, Joshua!" exclaimed Mrs. Lemington, spreading out the Billeville "Mirror" in her ample lap. "The *Nellie E. Williams* of Gloucester reports that she saw two whales, a cow and a calf, floating off Cape Cod the day before yesterday."

"Well, ma," replied old Mr. Lemington, "what's the matter with that?"

"Why, it's all right about the two whales, Joshua, but what bothers me is how the cow and the calf got way out there."

* * * * *

A Congressman once declared in an address to the House:

"As Daniel Webster says in his great dictionary—"

"It was Noah who wrote the dictionary," whispered a colleague, who sat at the next desk.

"Noah, nothing," replied the speaker. "Noah built the ark."

* * * * *

Father (who has been called upon in the city and asked for his daughter's hand)—"Louise, do you know what a solemn thing it is to be married?"

Louise—"Oh, yes, pa; but it is a good deal more solemn being single."

* * * * *

Captain Roald Amundsen, Norway's famous explorer, told this story about a National Guard encampment:

"A new volunteer, who had not quite learned his business, was on sentry duty, one night, when a friend brought him a pie from the canteen.

"As he sat on the grass eating pie, the major sauntered up in undress uniform. The sentry, not recognizing him, did not salute, and the major stopped and said:

"'What's that you have there?'

"'Pie,' said the sentry, good-naturedly. 'Apple pie. Have a bite?'

"The major frowned.

"'Do you know who I am?' he asked.

"'No,' said the sentry, 'unless you're the major's groom.'

"The major shook his head.

"'Guess again,' he growled.

"'The barber from the village?'

"'No.'

"'Maybe—' here the sentry laughed—'maybe you're the major himself?'

"'That's right. I am the major,' was the stern reply.

"The sentry scrambled to his feet.

"'Good gracious!' he exclaimed. 'Hold the pie, will you, while I present arms!'"

*****

A player for many years associated with the late Richard Mansfield relates that one day in Philadelphia, as he was standing by a huge poster in front of the theater a poster that represented Mansfield in the character of "Henry V.," a man who was strolling by stopped to gaze at the bill. Finally, with a snort of disgust, he muttered as he turned to go:

"'*Henry V.*—' what?"

*****

"There is an old negro down in my town," said John Sharp Williams, the former Democratic leader of the House, "who did me a service. I wanted to reward him, so I said:

"'Uncle, which shall I give you—a ton of coal or a bottle of whisky?'

"'Foh de Lo'd, Massa John,' he replied, 'you-all shorely knows I buhn wood.'"

*****

"No," remarked a determined lady to an indignant cabman who had received his legal fare, "you can not cheat me, my man. I haven't ridden in cabs for the last twenty-five years for nothing."

"Haven't you, mum?" replied the cabman, bitterly, gathering up the reins. "Well, you've done your best!"

*****

On the mighty deep.

The great ocean liner rolled and pitched.

"Henry," faltered the young bride, "do you still love me?"

"More than ever, darling!" was Henry's fervent answer.

Then there was eloquent silence.

"Henry," she gasped, turning her pale, ghastly face away. "I thought that would make me feel better, but it doesn't!"

*****

Once in Nice an Englishman and a Frenchman were about to separate on the Promenade des Anglais.

The Englishman, as he started toward the Cercle Mediterranee, called back:

"Au reservoir!"

And the Frenchman waved his hand and answered:

"Tanks."

* * * * *

During a Baptist convention held in Charleston the Rev. Dr. Greene of Washington strolled down to the Battery one morning to take a look across the harbor at Fort Sumter. An old negro was sitting on the seawall fishing. Dr. Greene watched the lone fisherman, and finally saw him pull up an odd-looking fish, a cross between a toad and a catfish.

"What kind of a fish is that, old man?" inquired Dr. Greene.

"Dey calls it de Baptist fish," replied the fisherman, as he tossed it away in deep disgust.

"Why do they call it the Baptist fish?" asked the minister.

"Because dey spoil so soon after dey comes outen de water," answered the fisherman.

* * * * *

Blanche, Wilbur, and Thomas were in the garden playing, and making a great deal of noise, but small Jack sat in a corner very quietly, which for Jack was an unusual proceeding. After watching them for some time, the mother's curiosity prompted her to ask:

"What are you playing?"

"We are playing house," answered Wilbur. "Blanche and I are the mother and father, and Thomas is the child."

"And what does Jack do?"

"Sh, sh! he isn't born yet."

* * * * *

Governor Chamberlain of Connecticut used to tell of an old friend who, because of his deafness, made some ludicrous and at times embarrassing mistakes. Once he was at a dinner party where the lady seated next to him tried to help him along in conversation. As the fruit was being passed, she asked him: "Do you like bananas?"

"No," said the old gentleman, with a look of mild surprise. "The fact is," he added in a confidential tone which could be heard in the next room, "I find the old-fashioned nightshirt is good enough for me."

* * * * *

An Atchison woman with a little baby tells the following story. She says that a woman caller said: "What a dear little baby; how old is it?" "Sixteen months," replied the Atchison woman. "Well, dear me, it looks older," said the caller, and then went on and talked and talked and finally turned again to the baby, and said: "That precious baby, how old is it?" "Sixteen months," replied the mother. "Well, dear me," smilingly said the caller. "Oh, such a big baby for its age," and went on talking and talking. Again turning to the baby the caller said: "What a darling angel the baby is; how old is it?" "Eighteen months," said the exasperated mother. "Well, I declare, it looks two years old," said the caller, and then talked and talked. Just as she was leaving the caller stooped and kissed the baby and said: "Bless its little heart; how old is it?" "Ten months," shrieked the outraged mother, but the caller tripped gaily away; she had not noticed the replies to her questions, and had no idea and did not care how old the baby was.

* * * * *

A boy went into a confectioner's shop and asked for a glass of lemonade. When it was given him he took it, looked at it, and said he would have a bun instead. The bun was given him; he ate it and was walking out of the shop when the confectioner called after him, "Hi, you haven't paid for your bun." "No," said the boy, "I gave you back the lemonade for that." "But," said the man, "you did not pay for the lemonade." "I didn't drink it," said the boy, and walked out of the shop leaving the confectioner calculating.

* * * * *

Two women overheard talking in a poor district of London: "Did ye ever 'ear tell of Lot's wife?" "Well, no, Mrs. Brown, I can't say I ever did. Why?" "Well, I don't know very much about 'er myself, but I 'ave 'eard tell of 'er that she turned into a pillar of salt." "Lord, did she? What funny things one does 'ear nowadays. It was only this morning I was out with my 'usband and 'e turned into a public-house."

* * * * *

Willie Green was not only chewing gum, but had his feet sprawled out in the aisle in a most unbecoming manner.

"Willie," said the teacher, "take that gum out of your mouth this instant, and put in your feet."

* * * * *

William was considered the brightest boy in his grade; upon hearing a lesson recited in class once or twice he knew it quite well. Thus, while the other fellows were compelled to study hard he scarcely found it necessary to open a book. At the expiration of the term one of the questions in the written geography was, "What is the equator?"

William, always to be depended upon, wrote without delay:

"The equator is a menagerie lion running around the center of the earth."

* * * * *

He was an earnest minister, and one Sunday, in the course of a sermon on the significance of little things, he said:

"The hand which made the mighty heavens made a grain of sand; which made the lofty mountains made a drop of water; which made you made the grass of the field; which made me made a daisy!"

* * * * *

A young Scotchman, bashful but desperately in love, finding no notice was taken of his visits to the house of his sweetheart, summoned up sufficient courage to address the fair one thus:

"Jean, I was here on Monday nicht."

"Ay, ye were that," replied she.

"An' I was here on Tuesday nicht."

"So ye were."

"An' I was here on Wednesday," continued the ardent youth.

"Ay, an' ye were on Thursday nicht an' a'."

"An' I was here last nicht."

"Weel," she says, "what if ye were?"

"An' I am here the nicht again."

"An' what about it even if ye came every nicht?"

"What about it, did ye say? Did ye no' begin to smell a rat?"

* * * * *

Rustic—"Well, Miss, I be fair mazed wi' the ways o' that 'ere fisherman—that I be!"

Parson's Daughter—"Why is that, Carver?"

Rustic—"The owd fool has been sittin' there for the last six hours and hasn't caught nothin'."

Parson's Daughter—"How do you know that?"

Rustic—"I've been a-watchin' o' he the whole time!"

* * * * *

A stately and venerable professor one morning, being unable to attend to his class on account of a cold, wrote on the blackboard:

"Dr. Dash, through indisposition, is unable to attend to his classes to-day."

The students erased one letter in this notice, making it read:

"Dr. Dash, through indisposition, is unable to attend to his lasses to-day."

But it happened a few minutes later that the professor returned for a box he had forgotten. Amid a roar of laughter he detected the change in his notice, and, approaching the blackboard, calmly erased one letter in his turn.

Now the notice read:

"Dr. Dash, through indisposition, is unable to attend to his asses to-day."

* * * * *

The man in the smoker was boasting of his unerring ability to tell from a man's looks exactly what city he came from. "You, for example," he said to the man next to him, "you are from New Orleans?" He was right.

"You, my friend," turning to the man on the other side of him, "I should say you are from Chicago?" Again he was right.

The other two men got interested.

"And you are from Boston?" he asked the third man.

"That's right, too," said the New Englander.

"And you from Philadelphia, I should say?" to the last man.

"No, sir," answered the man with considerable warmth; "I've been sick for three months: that's what makes me look that way!"

* * * * *

Five-year-old Nellie had been naughty all day. Finally her mama, a very portly woman, sat down and drew the little culprit across her ample lap to administer the long-delayed punishment. Nellie's face was fairly buried in the folds of her mother's dress. Before the maternal hand could descend Nellie turned her face to say, "Well, if I'm going to be spanked *I must have air.*"

* * * * *

"John," said the woman with nine chapeaux, "I got another new hat to-day." "My dear!" expostulated her husband, "that is the last straw." "I know it," she said; "just from Paris."

* * * * *

A prominent Bostonian inquired of a London shopkeeper for Hare's "Walks in London."

The shopkeeper, after much search, found it on his shelves, but in two volumes.

"Ah," said the Bostonian, "you have your Hare parted in the middle over here."

"What!" exclaimed the Englishman, blankly, passing his hands over his head.

* * * * *

Mr. Blaine used to tell this story: Once, in Dublin, toward the end of the opera, Mephistopheles was conducting Faust through a trap-door which represented the gates of hell. His majesty got through all right—he was used to going below—but Faust was quite stout, got half-way in, and no squeezing would get him any farther. Suddenly an Irishman in the gallery exclaimed devoutly: "Thank God! hell's full."

* * * * *

An Ohio man who was recently elected to Congress, went to Washington to look around and see what his duties were. He was hospitably received, and was wined and dined a great many times by his colleagues. Before he went home he said to his friends: "By George, I have had a good time! I have had dinners and breakfasts and suppers galore given to me. In fact, I haven't had my knife out of my mouth since I struck town."

* * * * *

When Commissioner Allen had charge of the Patent Office in Washington he was very punctilious about the respect due him and his position, and demanded full tribute from everybody.

One day, as he was sitting at his desk, two men came in without knocking or announcement and without removing their hats.

Allen looked up and impaled the intruders with his glittering eye. "Gentlemen," he said severely, "who are visitors to this office to see me are always announced, and always remove their hats."

"Huh," replied one of the men, "we ain't visitors, and we don't give a hoot about seeing you. We came in to fix the steam pipes."

* * * * *

One time there was a fire in a small town. It was being discussed in the hearing of several of the citizens. One man said he believed it was incendiary. Another replied: "Incendiary, nonsense! It was set on fire!"

* * * * *

Addressing a political gathering the other day a speaker gave his hearers a touch of the pathetic. "I miss," he said, brushing away a not unmanly tear, "I miss many of the old faces I used to shake hands with."

* * * * *

The Rev. Moses Jackson was holding services in a small country church, and at the conclusion lent his hat to a member (as was the custom) to pass around for contributions. The brother canvassed the congregation thoroughly, but the hat was returned empty to its owner.

Bre'r Jackson looked into it, turned it upside down, and shook it vigorously, but not a copper was forthcoming. He sniffed audibly. "Brederen," he said, "I sho' is glad dat I got my hat back ergin."

* * * * *

Pattern for all beneath the sun,
To Taft award the palm and bun!
They told him what they wanted done—
He done it.

* * * * *

Secretary Knox tells a good story of the last fight the late Senator Quay, of Pennsylvania, made in the Senate. Quay was working hard on the Oklahoma Statehood Bill, obstructing legislation, when a scheme was fixed up to get him away from the Senate for a time. Quay was very fond of tarpon fishing and had a winter place in Florida. One afternoon he received this telegram from a friend who thought the Senator might be in better business than pottering around about new States:

"Fishing never so good. Tarpon biting everywhere, sport magnificent; come."

Quay read the telegram and smiled a little smile. Then he answered:

"Tarpon may be biting, but I am not.—M. S. Quay."

* * * * *

"Now, children," said the teacher, "I want each of you to think of some animal or bird and try for the moment to be like the particular one you are thinking about, and make the same kind of noises they are in the habit of making."

Instantly the schoolroom became a menagerie. Lions roaring, dogs barking, birds singing and twittering, cows lowing, calves bleating, cats meowing, etc., all in an uproar and excitement—all with one exception, off in a remote corner a little fellow was sitting perfectly still, apparently indifferent and unmindful of the rest. The teacher observing him, approached and said: "Waldo, why are you not taking part with the other children?"

Waving her off with a deprecating hand and rebuking eyes he whispered: "Sh-sh-sh, teacher! I'm a rooster, and I'm a-layin' a aig!"

* * * * *

Bishop Brewster, of Connecticut, while visiting some friends not long ago, tucked his napkin in his collar to avoid the juice of the grapefruit at breakfast. He laughed as he did it, and said it reminded him of a man he once knew who rushed into a restaurant and, seating himself at a table, proceeded to tuck his napkin under his chin. He then called a waiter and said, "Can I get lunch here?" "Yes," responded the waiter in a dignified manner, "but not a shampoo."

* * * * *

A man and his wife were once staying at a hotel, when in the night they were aroused from their slumbers by the cry that the hotel was afire.

"Now, my dear," said the husband, "I will put into practise what I have preached. Put on all your indispensable apparel and keep cool."

Then he slipped his watch into his vest pocket and walked with his wife out of the hotel. When all danger was past, he said, "Now you see how necessary it is to keep cool."

The wife for the first time glanced at her husband.

"Yes, William," she said, "it is a grand thing, but if I were you I would have put on my trousers."

* * * * *

One evening as the mother of the little niece of Phillips Brooks was tucking her snugly in bed the maid stepped in and said there was a caller waiting in the parlor. The mother told the child to say her prayers and promised that she would be back in a few minutes.

The caller remained only a short time, and when the mother went upstairs again she asked the little girl if she had done as she was bidden.

"Yes, mama, I did and I didn't," she said.

"What do you mean by that, dear?"

"Well, mama, I was awfully sleepy, so I just asked God if he wouldn't excuse me to-night and He said, 'Oh, don't mention it, Miss Brooks.'"

* * * * *

"Would you mind walking the other w'y and not passing the 'orse?" said a London cabman with exaggerated politeness to the fat lady who had just paid a minimum fare.

"Why?" she inquired.

"Because if 'e sees wot 'e's been carryin' for a shilling 'e'll 'ave a fit."

* * * * *

One afternoon during a recent sea voyage of Ex-Ambassador Choate the waves were unpleasantly high, and the ship was rolling a bit, to the discomfiture of some passengers.

Mr. Choate remarked: "'Tis better to have lunched and lost than never to have lunched at all."

* * * * *

A certain minister was deeply impressed by an address on the evils of smoking given at a recent synod. He rose from his seat, went over to a fellow minister, and said:

"Brother, this morning I received a present of 100 good cigars. I have smoked one of them, but now I'm going home to burn the remainder in the fire."

The other minister arose, and said it was his intention to accompany his reverend brother.

"I mean to rescue the ninety and nine," he added.

* * * * *

Expecting a visit from the superintendent of an adjacent Sunday-school one Sunday afternoon, one enterprising teacher, anticipating the line of questions which would be asked of the scholars selected a boy from her class to answer each question. As she had figured it out, the visitor would first ask the pupils the question, "Who made you?" and the first pupil was, of course, to answer "God." The next question was to be "Of what?" to which the answer was to be "Of the dust of the earth." Unfortunately between the time that Sunday-school was called to order and the visiting superintendent took the floor, the first pupil was taken sick and obliged to go home. The teacher did not have the opportunity to readjust her forces, and when the first question was asked, the second boy thought it a good opportunity for him to get in his answer and have it off his mind; so to the question, "Who made you?" he answered, "Of the dust of the earth."

"Oh, no," said the visitor. "God made you."

"No, sir; He did not," said the youngster. "The little boy that God made has gone home sick, and I am the dust of the earth."

* * * * *

When General Grant was in London on his trip around the world he was invited to Windsor Castle by Queen Victoria. The queen received the party in one of the private audience chambers and chatted with General Grant for a few moments before dinner was served.

Jesse Grant, then a small boy, was with the general, and stood just behind him. As the general was talking, Jesse pulled impatiently at his coat-tails a number of times. Finally, the general turned half-way, and Jesse whispered:

"Pa, can't I be introduced?"

"Your Majesty," said the general, "I should like to present my son, Master Jesse."

The queen shook Jesse's hand cordially, and that young man, thinking it incumbent on him to say something, glanced approvingly around the room and said: "Fine house you have here, ma'am."

* * * * *

Daniel J. Sully, the former Cotton King, made a trip through the South one winter, and when he came back he told a story of an old negro who had been working for a cotton planter time out of mind. One morning he came to his employer and said:

"I'se gwineter quit, boss."

"What's the matter, Mose?"

"Well, sah, yer manager, Mistah Winter, ain't kicked me in de las' free mumfs."

"I ordered him not to kick you any more. I don't want anything like that around my place. I don't want any one to hurt your feelings, Mose."

"Ef I don't git any more kicks I'se goin' to quit. Ebery time Mistah Winter used ter kick and cuff me when he wuz mad he always git 'shamed of hisself and gimme a quarter. I'se done los' enuff money a'ready wid dis heah foolishness 'bout hurtin' ma feelin's."

* * * * *

A Chicago mistress had given the butcher her daily order over the telephone. Later in the day she decided to change it a little, and countermanded an order she had given for some liver.

Calling up the butcher, she said:

"You remember that I gave you an order this morning for a pound of liver?"

"Yes," answered the butcher.

"Well, I find that I can get along without it, and you need not send it."

Before she could put down the receiver she heard the butcher say to some one in the store:

"Cut out Mrs. Blank's liver. She says she can get along without it."

* * * * *

Tommy—"Ma, I met the minister on my way to Sunday-school and he asked me if I ever went fishing on Sunday."

Mother—"And what did you say, darling?"

Tommy—"I said, 'Get thee behind me, Satan,' and ran right away from him."

* * * * *

"My hair is falling out," admitted the timid man in the chemist's. "Can you recommend something to keep it in?"

"Certainly," replied the obliging assistant. "Here is a nice cardboard box."

* * * * *

An eloquent evangelist who was holding a series of protracted meetings had been interrupted on several occasions by the departure of some one of the audience. He determined to prevent further annoyance by making an example of the next one so doing. Therefore, when a young man arose to depart in the middle of a discourse, he said: "Young man, would you rather go to hell than listen to this sermon?" The individual addressed stopped midway up the aisle and, turning slowly about, answered: "Well, to tell the truth, I don't know but I would."

* * * * *

Mr. Seabury and his wife were on the point of moving to another flat. Both of them were anxious that the transfer should be made at the least possible expense, and the nearness of the new home promised materially to further this aim.

"I can carry loads of little things over in my brown bag," announced Mrs. Seabury. "And you can take books and so on in your big satchel."

In discussing further the matter of transportation, Mrs. Seabury remarked that, notwithstanding the heat, she could wear her winter coat over, and leave it, and return for her spring coat. The idea charmed her impractical husband.

"Why, I can do the same thing!" he said. "I'll wear over one suit and then come back for another!"

* * * * *

The ghost of Noah Webster came to a spiritual medium in Alabama, not long ago, and wrote on a slip of paper: "It is tite times." Noah was right, but we are sorry to see he has gone back on his dictionary.

* * * * *

Sydney Smith wrote to Jeffrey: "Tell Murray that I was much struck with the politeness of Miss Markham the day after he went. In carving a partridge I splashed her with gravy from head to foot; and, though I saw three distinct brown rills of juice trickling down her cheek, she had the complaisance to swear that not a drop had reached her. Such circumstances are the triumphs of civilized life."

* * * * *

During a certain battle the colonel of an Irish regiment noticed that one of his men was extremely devoted to him, and followed him everywhere. At length he remarked, "Well, my man, you have stuck by me well to-day."

"Yis, sorr," replied Pat. "Shure me mither said to me, said she, just stick to the colonel, Patrick, me bhoy, and you'll be all roight. Them colonels never gets hurted."

* * * * *

Miss Frances Keller, of the Woman's Municipal League of New York, illustrated admirably at a recent dinner party a point which she wished to make in reply to a man who had said, "Women are vainer than men."

"Of course," Miss Keller answered, "I admit that women are vain and men are not. There are a thousand proofs that this is so. Why, the necktie of the handsomest man in the room is even now up the back of his collar."

There were six men present and each of them put his hand gently behind his neck.

* * * * *

As father was leaving the house one morning he looked in vain for his umbrella.

"I expect sister's beau took it last night," ventured six-year-old Willie.

"Oh, you naughty boy," said Sister Mabel; "how can you say that?"

"Why, it's so," Willie insisted. "When he was saying good night I heard him say, 'I am going to steal just one!'"

* * * * *

During a conversation with a young lady Mark Twain had occasion to mention the word drydock.

"What is a drydock, Mr. Clemens?" she asked.

"A thirsty physician," replied the humorist.

* * * * *

Some officer had disobeyed or failed to comprehend an order. "I believe I'll sit down," said Secretary Stanton, "and give that man a piece of my mind."

"Do so," said Lincoln, "write him now while you have it on your mind. Make it sharp. Cut him all up." Stanton did not need a second invitation. It was a bone crusher that he read to the President.

"That's right," said Lincoln; "that's a good one."

"Whom can I send it by?" mused the Secretary.

"Send it!" replied Lincoln. "Why, don't send it at all. Tear it up. You have freed your mind on the subject, and that is all that is necessary. Tear it up. You never want to send such letters, I never do."

* * * * *

A certain old gentleman's lack of "polish" is a sad trial to his eldest daughter. Not long ago the family were gathered in the library, one of the windows of which was open.

"That air—" the father began, but was quickly interrupted.

"Father, dear, don't say 'that air'—say 'that there,'" the daughter admonished.

"Well, this ear—" he again attempted, but was as quickly brought to a halt.

"Nor 'this 'ere'; 'this here' is correct," he was told.

The old gentleman rose with an angry snort. "Look here, Mary," he said. "Of course I know you have been to school and all that, but I reckon I know what I want to say, an' I am going to say it. I believe I feel cold in this ear from that air, and I'm going to shut the window!"

* * * * *

"If you please, sir?"

"Well, Jimmy?"

"Me grandmother, sir—"

"Aha, your grandmother! Go on, Jimmy."

"Me grandmother an' me mother—"

"What, and your mother, too! Both very ill, eh?"

"No, sir. Me grandmother an' me mother are goin' to the baseball game this afternoon an' they want me to stay home an' take care of me little brudder."

* * * * *

Office-boy—"Please, Mr. Jones, my grandmother is dead, and so I must get off early to go to the funeral match—I mean the baseball ceremonies—that is—"

* * * * *

"That makes a difference," said Willie, snipping off the left ear of one of the twins.

* * * * *

Bill Nye, when a young man, made an engagement with a lady to take her driving. The appointed day came, but at the livery stable all the horses were taken save one old, shaky, exceedingly gaunt beast. Mr. Nye hired it and drove to his friend's residence. The lady kept him waiting over an hour before she was ready and then, viewing the shabby outfit, flatly refused to accompany Mr. Nye. "Why," she exclaimed, "that horse may die of old age any moment!"

"Madam," Mr. Nye replied, "when I arrived that horse was a prancing young colt."

* * * * *

In "Some Reminiscences" by William Rossetti is the following anecdote of Tennyson: "The witness was Allingham, to whom the incident happened. He was at breakfast at the house of the poet laureate, who, in a rather feeble moment of facetiousness, asked: 'Will you have a hegg?' 'Yes, thank you,' replied Allingham, who had scarcely appropriated the proffered viand when Tennyson added, 'I suppose you understand I was only joking when I said hegg?'"

* * * * *

"Long introductions when a man has a speech to make are a bore," said former Senator John C. Spooner, one of the great Senate leaders. "I have had all kinds, but the most satisfactory one in my career was that of a German mayor of a small town in my State, Wisconsin.

"I was to make a political address, and the opera-house was crowded. When it came time to begin, the mayor got up.

"'Mine friends,' he said, 'I hafe asked been to introduce Senator Spooner, who is to make a speech, yes. Veil, I haf dit so, und he vill now do so.'"

* * * * *

The "Outlook," of New York, tells a story of two church workers from a small town who came to New York on a slum hunt, and were more than satisfied. One of them was asked by a friend, on her return, where she and her husband had been. "In the slums of New York for a day and a night," she answered, enthusiastically. "My dear, it was hell upon earth. We had a *splendid* time!"

* * * * *

On one occasion a schoolmaster was very much annoyed by the conduct of a certain boy in his class. At last, finding the culprit giggling for no apparent reason, he cried indignantly, "Now, then, W., what are you laughing at? Are you laughing at me?" "No, sir," replied the astonished boy. "Then I don't see what else there is to laugh at," came the reply.

* * * * *

"Good by, Jessie!"

"Good by, Auntie May. I hope I'll be a great, big girl before you come to make us another visit."

* * * * *

The star pupil arose at the school entertainment to declaim his piece. "Lend me your ears!" he bawled. "Ha," sneered the mother of the opposition but defeated pupil, "that's Sarah Jane Doran's boy. He wouldn't be his mother's son if he didn't want to borrow something."

* * * * *

"While walking in one of the business thoroughfares of Pittsburg one year," says Robert Edeson, "my attention was arrested by a display of shirts in a haber-dasher's window, which for variety of sunset colors far excelled a Turner land-scape when the sun is red and low, and there in the window in glaring green type a large sign read, 'Listen!'"

* * * * *

One of a party of gentlemen left his corner seat in an already crowded railway car to go in search of something to eat, leaving a rug to reserve his place. On return-ing he found that in spite of the rug and the protests of his fellow passengers, the seat had been usurped by a woman clad in handsome clothes. With flashing eyes she turned upon him: "Do you know, sir, that I am one of the directors' wives?" "Madam," he replied, "were you the director's only wife I should still protest."

* * * * *

Mr. C., a distinguished lawyer of Boston, was on his way to Denver to transact some important business. During the afternoon he noticed, in the opposite section of the Pullman, a sweet-faced, tired-appearing woman traveling with four small children. Being fond of children and feeling sorry for the mother, he soon made friends with the little ones.

Early the next morning he heard their eager questions and the patient "Yes, dear," of the mother as she tried to dress them, and looking out he saw a small white foot protruding beyond the opposite curtain. Reaching across the aisle, he took hold of the large toe and began to recite: "This little pig went to market; this little pig stayed at home; this little pig had roast beef; this little pig had none; this little pig cried wee wee all the way home." The foot was suddenly withdrawn and a cold, quiet voice said: "That is quite sufficient, thank you."

Mr. C. hastily withdrew to the smoker, where he remained until the train ar-rived in Denver.

* * * * *

"'Deed I am going to get married," said little Winnie, the bright daughter of a tenant on a quiet farm in a quiet county in "The Northern Neck" of Virginia.

"I don't believe anybody will have you," said Miss Mabel, the landlord's daughter, teasingly.

"Yes, they will; I'll make 'em," said Winnie. "I'm going to get married and have *five* children—two of 'em colored," thoughtfully, "to do my work."

* * * * *

A reverend gentleman was addressing a Sunday-school class not long ago, and was trying to enforce the doctrine that when people's hearts were sinful they needed regulating. Taking out his watch, and holding it up, he said:

"Now, here is my watch; suppose it doesn't keep good time—now goes too fast, and now too slow—what shall I do with it?"

"Sell it," promptly replied a boy.

* * * * *

The high-born dame was breaking in a new footman—stupid but honest.

In her brougham, about to make a round of visits, she found she had forgotten her bits of pasteboard. So she sent the lout back with orders to bring some of her cards that were on the mantelpiece in her boudoir, and put them in his pocket.

Here and there she dropped one and sometimes a couple, until at last she told Jeames to leave three.

"Can't do it, mum."

"How's that?"

"I've only got two left—the ace of spades and the seven of clubs!"

* * * * *

The small son of a certain university professor, whose parents are deservedly popular for their tact and courteous speech, appeared at the home of a fellow professor and hesitatingly asked Mrs. X. if he might look at the parlor rug. Permission was, of course, granted, and Mrs. X. felt some surprise to see the little fellow stoop over the rug and stare silently for some half-minute. He straightened himself up and, meeting her wondering expression, said triumphantly:

"It doesn't make *me* sick!"

* * * * *

Uncle Harry was a bachelor and not fond of babies. Even winsome four-year-old Helen failed to win his heart. Every one made too much fuss over the youngster, Uncle Harry declared.

One day Helen's mother was called downstairs and with fear and trembling asked Uncle Harry, who was stretched out on a sofa, if he would keep his eye on Helen. Uncle Harry grunted "Yes," but never stirred from his position—in truth his eyes were tight shut.

By-and-by wee Helen tiptoed over to the sofa and leaning over Uncle Harry softly inquired:

"Feepy?"

"No," growled Uncle Harry.

"Tired?" ventured Helen.

"No," said her uncle.

"Sick?" further inquired Helen, with real sympathy in her voice.

"No," still insisted Uncle Harry.

"Dus' feel bum, hey?"

And that won the uncle!

* * * * *

A member of the faculty of the University of Wisconsin tells of some amusing replies made by a pupil undergoing an examination in English. The candidate had been instructed to write out examples of the indicative, the subjunctive, the potential, and the exclamatory moods. His effort resulted as follows:

"I am endeavoring to pass an English examination. If I answer twenty questions I shall pass. If I answer twelve questions I may pass. God help me!"

* * * * *

A clergyman was very anxious to introduce some hymn-books into the church, and arranged with his clerk that the latter was to give out the notice immediately after the sermon. The clerk, however, had a notice of his own to give out with reference to the baptism of infants. Accordingly, at the close of the sermon he arose and announced that "All those who have children whom they wish to have baptized please send in their names at once to the clerk." The clergyman, who was stone deaf, assumed that the clerk was giving out the hymn-book notice, and immediately rose and said: "And I should say, for the benefit of those who haven't any, that they may obtain some from the ushers any day from three to four o'clock; the ordinary little ones at twenty-five cents each, and special ones at fifty cents."

* * * * *

Clyde Fitch, the brilliant playwright, said of a jeweled watch that had been sent him by a Scotch admirer in Peebles:

"A jeweled watch from Peebles. How strangely unexpected! It reminds me of an open-air performance of 'As You Like It' that I once rehearsed.

"I rehearsed this amateur performance in a garden that was overlooked by a building operation. As my amateurs postured and chanted the bard's beautiful lines, bricklayers above us laid bricks, carpenters planed boards, and masons chipped stones.

"And one afternoon, during a silent pause in our rehearsal, we heard a voice from the building operation say gravely:

"'I prithee, malapert, pass me yonder brick.'"

* * * * *

A clergyman who was very popular with his congregation saw a lady about to call whom he was anxious not to meet. So he said to his wife:

"I'll run upstairs, my dear, and escape till she goes away."

After about an hour he quietly tiptoed to the stair landing and listened. All was quiet below. Reassured, he began to descend, and called out over the balustrade:

"Well, my dear, you got rid of that old bore at last?"

The next instant a voice from below rooted him to the spot. It was the voice of the caller! Then came a response which sounded inexpressibly sweet to him. It was the voice of his wife:

"Yes, dear, she went away over an hour ago; but here is our good friend, Mrs. Blank, whom I am sure you want to meet."

* * * * *

A lady and her little daughter were walking through a fashionable street when they came to a portion of the street strewn with straw, so as to deaden the noise of vehicles passing a certain house.

"What's that for, ma?" said the child, to which the mother replied, "The lady who lives in that house, my dear, has had a little baby girl sent her." The child thought a moment, looked at the quantity of straw, and said: "Awfully well packed, wasn't she, ma?"

* * * * *

A politician, upon his arrival at one of the small towns in North Dakota, where he was to make a speech the following day, found that the two so-called hotels were crowded to the doors.

Not having telegraphed for accommodations, the politician discovered that he would have to make shift as best he could.

He was compelled for that night to sleep on a wire cot which had only some blankets and a sheet on it. As the statesman is a fat man, he found his improvised bed anything but comfortable.

"Well," asked a friend, when the politician appeared in the dining-room in the morning, "how did you sleep?"

"Oh, fairly well," replied the statesman, nonchalantly, "but I looked like a waffle when I got up."

* * * * *

William Waldorf Astor, before he set out for his English home, said, apropos of the Russo-Japanese War: "Nations engaged in war not only harm each other, but they lay themselves open to harm at the hands of all sorts of other nations. In fact, two nations at war are in the defenseless and gullible position of a certain English married couple.

"This couple will fall out and cease to speak to one another for a year or more at a time. They have a beautiful country house, and there is a certain elderly matron, a great bore, who visits them continually. Some one asked this matron which of the pair was always inviting her. She answered, frankly, 'Neither invites me ever, but since they don't speak to each other, each always thinks I am the other's guest.'"

* * * * *

They were talking over the carelessness of well-to-do people who, by overlooking their small bills, frequently bring disaster upon the tradesmen who are trying to do business on a small capital.

"It sometimes happens that these poor devils have two or three times the amount of their capital out in bills that if paid promptly would make their commercial ways a path of roses," said the economist. "Little bills of three, four, and five dollars, not much in themselves, mount up high in the aggregate, and it sometimes happens that a seeming prosperity, through the failure of a lot of customers to pay their bills within a reasonable time, results in ruin.

"And yet," said the reminiscencer, "it sometimes works the other way. I heard a story in England once of a harness dealer who on entering his shop one afternoon, after an absence of several hours, noticed that a rather handsome saddle that he had had in stock had disappeared. He made immediate inquiry of his salesmen, and one of them informed him that he had sold it to a gentleman who had come to the shop with his trap, that the purchaser had thrown it into his wagon and driven off, after telling him to charge it. Unfortunately, however, he had forgotten to ask the gentleman's name, and all effort to identify him by description failed.

"'Well,' said the shopkeeper, who was an ingenious man, 'there is only one thing left to be done. We will charge the saddle up on all our outstanding accounts. Those who did not buy the saddle will, of course, call our attention to our error, and the man who did take it will, of course, pay.'

"This method was adopted, and at the beginning of the next month the bills were sent out accordingly. Two weeks later the saddler approached his cashier, and asked if he had heard as yet about the matter. 'How about that missing saddle, Marcus?' he asked. 'We are doing very well, sir,' replied the cashier. 'Forty of our customers have paid for it, and only two have discovered the mistake.'"

* * * * *

The story is told of a young Oregon girl, a favorite in society, but who was poor and had to take care not to get her evening gowns soiled, as their number was limited. At a dance not long ago a great, big, red-faced, perspiring man came in and asked her to dance. He wore no gloves. She looked at the well-meaning moist hands despairingly, and thought of the immaculate back of her waist. She hesitated a bit, and then she said, with a winning smile:

"Of course I will dance with you, but if you don't mind, won't you please use your handkerchief?"

The man looked at her blankly a moment or two. Then a light broke over his face.

"Why, certainly," he said.

And he pulled out his handkerchief and blew his nose.

* * * * *

Willie finally persuaded his aunt to play train with him. The chairs were arranged in line and then he said:

"Now, you be engineer and I'll be the conductor. Lend me your watch and get up into your cab." He then hurried down the platform, timepiece in hand.

"Pull out there, you red-headed, pie-faced jay," he shouted to the astonished young woman.

"Why, Willie," she exclaimed in amazement.

"That's right, chew the rag," he retorted. "Pull out. We're five minutes late already."

They have had to forbid his playing down by the tracks.

* * * * *

Andrew Lang once wrote to Israel Zangwill to ask him to take part in an author's reading for the benefit of a charity, and received in reply the following laconic message: "If A. Lang will—I. Zangwill."

* * * * *

Mr. Peet, a rather diffident man, was unable to prevent himself from being introduced one evening to a fascinating young lady, who, misunderstanding his name, constantly addressed him as Mr. Peters, much to the gentleman's distress. Finally, summoning courage, he bashfully but earnestly remonstrated:

"Oh, don't call me Peters; call me Peet!"

"Ah, but I don't know you well enough, Mr. Peters," said the young lady, blushing as she playfully withdrew behind her fan.

* * * * *

Senator Tillman, of South Carolina, tells of a little girl whose statements were always exaggerated until she became known in school and Sunday-school as a "little liar." Her parents were dreadfully worried about her, and made strenuous efforts to correct the bad habit. One afternoon her mother overheard an argument with her playmate. Willie Bangs, who seemed to finish the discussion by saying emphatically: "I'm older than you, 'cause my birthday comes first, in May, and yours don't come until September."

"Oh, of course your birthday comes first," sneeringly answered little Nellie; "but that is 'cause you came down first. I remember looking at the angels when they were making you."

"Come here, Nellie; come here instantly," cried her mother. "It is breaking mother's heart," said she, "to hear you tell such awful stories. Remember what happened to Ananias and Sapphira, don't you?"

"Oh, yes, mama, I know. They were struck dead for lying. I saw them carried into the corner drugstore."

* * * * *

The relationship between Mr. Gladstone and his wife was one of the most beautiful the world has known, and of all the millions who looked up to him, she was his greatest admirer. On one occasion when Mrs. Gladstone was entertaining visitors, conversation turned on the Bible, and there was a lively argument on the meaning of a certain passage.

Presently one of the callers, hoping to end the discussion, remarked devoutly:

"There is One alone who knows all."

The cloud vanished from Mrs. Gladstone's face and she smiled sunnily as she said:

"Yes, and William will be down in a few minutes."

* * * * *

Mabel (testing the wisdom of the grown-ups).—"Well, how did Martin Luther die?"

Uncle Jim.—"Die? Oh, in the ordinary way, I suppose."

Mabel.—"Oh, Uncle! you really don't know anything. He was excommunicated by a bull."

* * * * *

Small Robbie was laboring over a drawing which was obviously of great importance.

His mother, who was sewing in the room, got up to see what he was doing.

"What is it you're drawing, dear?" she said, as she stood behind him.

Robbie was embarrassed. Struggling to cover his nervousness, he answered with an air of great nonchalance:

"Oh, it's papa I'm drawing, but I don't care anything about it. Guess I'll put a tail to it, and have it for a dog."

* * * * *

It is told of Charles Lamb, that one afternoon, returning from a dinner-party, having taken a seat in a crowded omnibus, a stout gentleman subsequently looked in, and politely asked, "All full inside?" "I don't know how it may be with the *other* passengers," answered Lamb, "but that last piece of oyster-pie did the business for *me*."

* * * * *

One of the ladies-in-waiting to the late Queen Victoria had a very bright little daughter about four years old of whom the Queen was very fond.

The Queen invited the child to have lunch with her.

Of course the mother was highly pleased, and charged the little girl to be very careful about her table manners, and to be very polite and careful before the Queen.

The little girl came home in high glee, and the mother asked her all about the luncheon.

"Were you a very polite little girl? and did you remember to do all I told you at the table?" asked the proud mama.

"Oh, yes. I was polite," said the little one, "but the Queen wasn't."

"The Queen wasn't!" said the mother. "Why, what did she do?"

"She took her chicken bone up in her fingers, and I just shook my finger at her like you did at me, and said, 'Piggy, piggy, piggy!'"

* * * * *

A young girl once asked Mark Twain if he liked books for Christmas gifts.

"Well, that depends," drawled the great humorist. "If a book has a leather cover it is really valuable as a razor strop. If it is a brief, concise work, such as the French write, it is useful to put under the short leg of a wabbly table. An old-fashioned book with a clasp can't be beat as a missile to hurl at a dog, and a large book like a geography is as good as a piece of tin to nail over a broken pane of glass."

* * * * *

One of the most candid tributes the late Edwin Booth ever received was rendered to him on his last Southern tour by one who knew neither of his presence nor of his identity in the play. Mr. Booth told the story to his friend, Dr. John H. Girdner.

"We opened our engagement in Atlanta, Ga., with 'Othello,'" said Mr. Booth, "and I played Othello. After the performance my friend, Mr. Malone, and I went to the Kimball House for some refreshment. The long bar was so crowded that we had to go around the corner of it before we could find a vacant space. While we were waiting to be served we couldn't help hearing the conversation of two fine-looking old boys, splendid old fellows with soft hats, flowing mustaches, and chin tufts, black string ties and all the other paraphernalia.

"'I didn't see you at the theater this evening, Cunnel,' said one.

"'No,' replied the other. 'I didn't buy seats till this mawnin', and the best we could get were six rows back in the balcony. I presume, suh, you were in the orchestra.'

"'Yes, Cunnel, I was in the orchestra,' said the first man. 'Madam and the girls were with me. We all agreed that we nevuh attended a mo' thrillin' play. The company was good, too, excellent company. And do you know, Gunnel, in my opinion that d—d nigguh did about as well as any of 'em!'"

* * * * *

A Southern colonel had a colored valet by the name of George. George received nearly all of the colonel's cast-off clothing. He had his eyes on a certain pair of light trousers which were not wearing out fast enough to suit him, so he thought he would hasten matters somewhat by rubbing grease on one knee. When the colonel saw the spot, he called George and asked if he had noticed it. George said, "Yes, sah, Colonel, I noticed dat spot and tried mighty hard to git it out, but I couldn't."

"Have you tried gasoline?" the colonel asked.

"Yes, sah, Colonel, but it didn't do no good."

"Have you tried brown paper and a hot iron?"

"Yes, sah, Colonel, I'se done tried 'mos' everything I knows of, but dat spot wouldn't come out."

"Well, George, have you tried ammonia?" the colonel asked as a last resort.

"No, sah, Colonel, I ain't tried 'em on yet, but I knows dey'll fit."

* * * * *

It was the first vaudeville performance the old colored lady had ever seen, and she was particularly excited over the marvelous feats of the magician. But when he covered a newspaper with a heavy flannel cloth and read the print through it, she grew a little nervous. He then doubled the cloth and again read the letters accurately.

This was more than she could stand, and rising in her seat, she said:

"I'm goin' home. This ain't no place for a lady in a thin calico dress!"

* * * * *

At a certain railway junction the train divides, one portion going to Edinburgh, the other to Glasgow. The guard put his head in at one of the carriage windows and asked, "All here for Edinburgh?" All replied in the affirmative except one old woman, who after the train had started remarked with a smile, "I was just goin' to Glesca masel' but I wasna goin' to tell yon inquisitive deevil."

* * * * *

A pompous Bishop of Oxford was once stopped on a London street by a ragged urchin.

"Well, my little man, what can I do for you?" inquired the churchman. "The time o' day, please, your lordship."

With considerable difficulty the portly Bishop extracted his watch. "It is exactly half-past five, my lad."

"Well," said the boy, setting his feet for a good start, "at 'alf-past six you go to 'ell!" and he was off like a flash and around the corner. The Bishop, flushed and furious, his watch dangling from its chain, floundered wildly after him. But as he rounded the corner he ran plump into the outstretched arms of the venerable Bishop of London.

"Oxford, Oxford," remonstrated that surprised dignitary, "why this unseemly haste?"

Puffing, blowing, spluttering, the outraged Bishop gasped out: "That young ragamuffin—I told him it was half-past five—and—he—er—told me to go to hell at half-past six."

"Yes, yes," said the Bishop of London with a twinkle in his kindly old eyes, "but why such haste? You've got almost an hour."

* * * * *

A lady entered a railway station not a hundred miles from Edinburgh and said she wanted a ticket for London. The pale-looking clerk asked:

"Single?"

"It ain't any of your business," she replied. "I might have been married a dozen times if I'd felt like providin' for some poor shiftless wreck of a man like you."

* * * * *

"M-my dear," said the muddled citizen, "I 'sure you I wouldn't been s'late, but footpad stopped me."

"And you were so scared your tongue clove to the roof of your mouth."

"How'd you know that?"

"I smell the clove."

* * * * *

A man addicted to walking in his sleep went to bed all right one night, but when he awoke he found himself on the street in the grasp of a policeman. "Hold on," he cried, "you mustn't arrest me. I'm a somnambulist." To which the policeman replied: "I don't care what your religion is—yer can't walk the streets in yer nightshirt."

* * * * *

"I can't keep the visitors from coming up," said the office-boy dejectedly to the editor. "When I say you're out they don't believe me. They say they must see you."

"Well," said the editor, "just tell them that's what they all say. I don't care if you 'cheek' them, but I must have quietness."

That afternoon there called at the office a lady. She wanted to see the editor, and the boy assured her that it was impossible.

"But I must see him!" she protested. "I'm his wife!"

"That's what they all say," replied the boy. And forthwith a new boy was wanted there.

* * * * *

Mr. Weedon Grossmith used to tell a good story about a play by Mr. Robert Ganthony, which that gentleman asked him to read. Mr. Grossmith took the comedy, but lost it on his way home. "Night after night," he said, "I would meet Ganthony and he would ask me how I liked his play. It was awful; the perspiration used to come out on my forehead as I'd say sometimes, 'I haven't had time to look at it yet!' or again, 'The first act was good, but I can't stop to explain,' etc., 'must catch a train.' That play was the bane of my existence, and haunted me even in my dreams." Some months passed, and Ganthony, a merry wag, still pursued him without mercy. At last it occurred to Mr. Grossmith that he might have left the comedy in the cab on the night it was given to him. He inquired at Scotland Yard.

"Oh! yes," was the reply. "Play marked with Mr. Ganthony's name, sent back to owner four months ago, as soon as found."

* * * * *

Some years ago when Head Consul Book, of the Western Jurisdiction, Woodmen of the World, was traveling through the South, the train stopped for some time in a small town, and Mr. Book alighted to make a purchase. The storekeeper could not make the correct change for the bill which was presented, so Mr. Book started in search of some one who could.

Sitting beside the door, whittling a stick, was an old darky.

"Uncle," said Mr. Book, "can you change a ten-dollar bill?" The old fellow looked up in surprise; then he touched his cap, and replied: "'Deed, an' Ah can't, boss, but Ah' 'preciates de honah, jest de same."

* * * * *

A gentleman riding with an Irishman came within sight of an old gallows and, to display his wit, said:

"Pat, do you see that?"

"To be sure Oi do," replied Pat.

"And where would you be to-day if the gallows had its due?"

"Oi'd be riding alone," replied Pat.

* * * * *

Jerry O'Rafferty came from the north of Ireland. During all his life there and later in Chicago he had never been inside a Catholic Church.

He was something of a scoffer at religious ceremonies, although he knew little about them. His good friend, Michael O'Brien, was troubled at this, and always used his influence to get Jerry into the church. At last he was successful. Jerry grudgingly consented to go to church Easter Sunday because of the importance of the occasion.

The two sat together, Jerry an interested spectator, while Mike entered into the services like the devout man he was.

Jerry was soon evidently impressed by the splendor of his surroundings and the grandeur of the services. He watched the lighting of the candles and listened attentively to the glorious burst of Easter music. Then he could refrain from commenting no longer.

"Mike," he whispered, leaning over to his companion, "this bates h—l."

"Whist," replied Mike, in a loud whisper, "sich is the intintion."

* * * * *

Bishop Wilmer of Alabama, famous as a story-teller, told of one of his friends who had lost a dearly beloved wife and, in his sorrow, caused these words to be inscribed on her tombstone: "The light of mine eyes has gone out." The bereaved married within a year. Shortly afterward the Bishop was walking through the graveyard with another gentleman. When they arrived at the tomb, the latter asked the Bishop what he would say of the present state of affairs, in view of the words on the tombstone. "I think," said the Bishop, "the words 'But I have struck another match' should be added."

* * * * *

A man of letters who visited Washington recently appeared at but one dinner-party during his stay. Then he sat next to the daughter of a noted naval officer. Her vocabulary is of a kind peculiar to very young girls, but she rattled away at the famous man without a moment's respite. It was during a pause in the general conversation that she said to him: "I'm awfully stuck on Shakespeare. Don't you think he's terribly interesting?" Everybody listened to hear the great man's brilliant reply, for as a Shakespearian scholar he has few peers. "Yes," he said, solemnly, "I do think he is interesting. I think he is more than that. I think Shakespeare is just simply too cute for anything."

* * * * *

A well-known Scotch professor was occasionally called up to Balmoral to attend the late Queen Victoria, and was extremely proud of the honor. One day a notice appeared in the university which stated that Professor — — could not attend his classes that day as he had been called up to Balmoral to see the Queen. A waggish student who saw the notice wrote underneath it, "God save the Queen."

* * * * *

"The other day," said a man passenger in a street-car, "I saw a woman in a street-car open a satchel and take out a purse, close the satchel and open the purse, take out a dime and close the purse, open the satchel and put in the purse. Then she gave the dime to the conductor and took a nickel in exchange. Then she opened the satchel and took out the purse, closed the satchel and opened the purse, put in the nickel and closed the purse, opened the satchel and put in the purse, closed the satchel and locked both ends. Then she felt to see if her back hair was all right, and it was all right, and she was all right. That was a woman."

* * * * *

As a couple of callers were in the parlor of a friend who is a firm Christian Scientist, the voice of five-year-old Florence could be heard from an upper room, fretting. Upon their inquiries about her the mother replied simply she was suffering from a "belief" in a boil.

One of the visitors was a rather grim great-aunt of the family who possesses a most lively scorn of Mrs. Eddy's so-called science as well as a deep-rooted affection for little Florence. She immediately demanded what had been applied for her relief and as naturally the answer was, "Nothing." She assumed her most decided expression, drew off her gloves and started upstairs.

"Aunt Molly, what are you going to do? I must repeat it is only a belief in a boil," expostulated the mother.

"Very well," retorted Aunt Molly, continuing her march upstairs, "I am merely going to put on a dream of a poultice."

And she did.

* * * * *

Mistress—"Did the fisherman who stopped here this morning have frog's legs?"

Nora—"Sure, mum, I dinnaw. He wore pants."

* * * * *

When the thermometer dropped below zero Mrs. Rogers was much disturbed by the thought that Huldah, the new kitchen maid, slept in an unheated room.

"Huldah," she said, remembering the good old custom of her girlhood, "it's going to be pretty cold to-night. I think you had better take a flatiron to bed with you."

"Yes, ma'am," assented Huldah without enthusiasm.

Mrs. Rogers, happy in the belief that her maid was comfortable, slept soundly. In the morning she visited the kitchen.

"Well, Huldah, how did you get along with the flatiron?"

Huldah breathed a deep sigh of recollection.

"Vell, ma'am, I got it 'most warm before morning."

* * * * *

Many children are so crammed with everything that they really know nothing.

In proof of this, read these veritable specimens of definitions, written by public-school children:

"Stability is taking care of a stable."

"A mosquito is the child of black and white parents."

"Monastery is the place for monsters."

"Tocsin is something to do with getting drunk."

"Expostulation is to have the smallpox."

"Cannibal is two brothers who killed each other in the Bible."

"Anatomy is the human body, which consists of three parts, the head, the chist, and the stummick. The head contains the eyes and brains, if any. The chist contains the lungs and a piece of the liver. The stummick is devoted to the bowels, of which there are five, a, e, i, o, u, and sometimes w and y."

* * * * *

Little Polly, coming in from her walk one morning, informed her mother that she had seen a lion in the park. No amount of persuasion or reasoning could make her vary her statement one hairbreadth. That night, when she slipped down on her knees to say her prayers, her mother said, "Polly, ask God to forgive you for that fib."

Polly hid her face for a moment. Then she looked straight into her mother's eyes, her own eyes shining like stars, and said, "I did ask him, mama, dearest, and he said, 'Don't mention it, Miss Polly; that big yellow dog has often fooled me.'"

* * * * *

"Boohoo! Boohoo!" wailed little Johnny.

"Why, what's the matter, dear?" his mother asked comfortingly.

"Boohoo—er—p-picture fell on papa's toes."

"Well, dear, that's too bad, but you mustn't cry about it, you know."

"I d-d-didn't. I l-laughed. Boohoo! Boohoo!"

* * * * *

Two candidates for office in Missouri were stumping the northern part of the State. In one town their appearance was almost simultaneous. The candidate last arriving stopped at a house for a drink of water. To the little girl who answered his knock at the door he said—when she had given him the desired drink and he had offered her some candy in recompense:

"Did the man ahead of me give you anything?"

"Oh, yes," replied the girl. "He gave me candy."

"Ah!" exclaimed the candidate. "Here's five cents for you. I don't suppose that *he* gave you any money?"

The youngster laughed. "Yes, he did, too! He gave me ten cents!"

Not to be outdone, the candidate gave the little one another nickel and picking her up in his arms, kissed her.

"Did he kiss you, too?" he asked genially.

"Yes, he did, sir," responded the little girl, "and he kissed ma, too."

* * * * *

The owner of a dry-goods store heard a new clerk say to a customer, "No, madam, we have not had any for a long time."

With a fierce glance at the clerk the smart employer rushed up to the woman and said: "We have plenty of everything in reserve ma'am; plenty upstairs."

The customer and the clerk looked dazed. Then the proprietor, seeing that something was wrong, said to the customer: "Excuse me, what did you ask for?"

The woman simply replied, "Why, I said to your clerk that we hadn't had any rain lately."

* * * * *

Senator W. A. Clark detests nothing more than to be interrupted when busy. One day he was in his office engaged in a business conversation when a petite woman, carrying a black bag, entered. With a compelling smile and an insinuating manner she approached the surly millionaire. Utterly insensible to his repellent mood and indifferent to his abrupt manner she drew from the depths of a bag a handsomely bound volume, the merits and beauty of which she began eloquently to descant upon.

Failing to embarrass her with arctic frigidity and impatient at her persistency under rebuffs all but vulgar, he turned suddenly upon the chattering woman and asked:

"Madam, do you know what my time is worth?"

She confessed it was a conundrum.

"Well," he said, petulantly, "it's worth $30 an hour!"

He turned away with the air of one who had settled the matter definitely beyond any further controversy. But he didn't know the woman.

"Oh, I'm so grateful to you, Mr. Clark," she replied, with a tone of pathos in her voice. "Thirty dollars an hour, did you say?"

"Yes; that's what I said, and it's cheap at that," and he smiled cynically.

"Oh, I know it's dirt cheap," she chirped with winsome blitheness. "I am so glad you told me"—rummaging in her reticule, from which she quickly flashed out a purse gorged with currency. Moving near to the astonished millionaire, who now regarded her movements with unfeigned curiosity, she counted two bills, a ten and a five, off the roll. These she pushed along the top of the sloping desk toward him and said: "Yes, I'm glad you told me, because I hadn't expected to get it so cheap. There is $15. Now, I want a half hour of your uninterrupted attention while I talk to you about this book."

Clark pushed the money back and subscribed and paid for two copies of the book.

* * * * *

The following bit from a letter of thanks is cherished by its recipient: "The beautiful clock you sent us came in perfect condition, and is now in the parlor on top of the book-shelves, where we hope to see you soon, and your husband, also, if he can make it convenient."

* * * * *

Tourist (in French restaurant)—"This is awful! I've ordered three dishes from this menu and they are all potatoes!"

* * * * *

"Mistah Brown," said the old colored woman, coming into the cross-roads store, "you ain't got no spool-cotton number thirty, is you?"

"Why, aunt Sally, I didn't say I didn't have it, did I?"

"You go long, Mistah Brown. I didn't ax you 'aint you got it?' I axed you 'is you'?—ain't you?"

* * * * *

An old "befo-de-wah" darky was called upon to make a few remarks over the grave of a friend. He removed his hat and stepped reverently and sadly toward the open grave and in solemn funereal tones said: "Friday Vizer, you is gone. We hope you is gone whar we spects you ain't!"

* * * * *

A New Yorker who does his bit of "globe trotting" tells of two odd entries that he saw in the visitors' book of a fashionable resort on the Rhine.

A few years ago one of the Paris members of the Rothschild family had registered as follows:

"R. de Paris."

It chanced that the next visitor to inscribe his name in the book was Baron Oppenheim, the banker of Cologne, and he wrote beneath Rothschild's:

"O. de Cologne."

* * * * *

The Stranger—"And who are the Murphys' ancestors?"

Mr. M.—"Ancestors? What's that?"

The Stranger—"I mean who do the Murphys spring from?"

Mr. M.—"The Murphys spring from no one. They spring *at* thim!"

* * * * *

At a wedding-feast recently the bridegroom was called upon, as usual, to respond to the given toast, in spite of the fact that he had previously pleaded to be excused. Blushing to the roots of his hair, he rose to his feet. He intended to imply that he was unprepared for speechmaking, but he unfortunately placed his hand upon his bride's shoulder, and looked down at her as he stammered out his opening and concluding words:

"This—er—thing has been forced upon me."

* * * * *

Very much excited and out of breath, a young man who could not have been married very long rushed up to an attendant at one of the city hospitals and inquired after Mrs. Brown, explaining between breaths that it was his wife whom he felt anxious about.

The attendant looked at the register and replied that there was no Mrs. Brown in the hospital.

"My God! Don't keep me waiting in this manner," said the excited young man. "I must know how she is."

"Well, she isn't here," again said the attendant.

"She must be," broke in the visitor, "for here is a note I found on the kitchen-table when I came home from work."

The note read:

"*Dear Jack*—Have gone to have my kimono cut out. ANNIE."

* * * * *

While an Irishman was gazing in the window of a Washington bookstore the following sign caught his eye:

DICKENS' WORKS
ALL THIS WEEK FOR
ONLY $4.00.

"The divvle he does!" exclaimed Pat in disgust. "The dirty scab!"

* * * * *

A dear old New England spinster, the embodiment of the timid and shrinking, passed away at Carlsbad, where she had gone for her health. Her nearest kinsman, a nephew, ordered her body sent back to be buried—as was her last wish—in the quiet little country churchyard. His surprise can be imagined, when on opening the casket, he beheld, instead of the placid features of his aunt Mary, the majestic port of an English General in full regimentals, whom he remembered had chanced to die at the same time and place as his aunt.

At once he cabled to the General's heirs explaining the situation and requesting instructions.

They came back as follows: "Give the General quiet funeral. Aunt Mary interred to-day with full military honors, six brass bands, saluting guns."

* * * * *

Early in the morning session, when the pupils were feeling bright and happy, the teacher thought it a good plan to give them sentences to correct, both as to grammar and sense. She accordingly wrote on the blackboard: "The hen has four legs. He done it." Thoughtful little Ignatius, at the foot of the class, pondered deeply, and at the end of the fifteen minutes' time allowed for correction he wrote: "*He* didn't done it: God done it."

* * * * *

The late John Stetson, famous in his day as a theatrical manager, was having a yacht built, and a friend, meeting him on the street, asked him what he was going to name the boat. "I haven't decided yet," replied John, "but it will be some name commencing with S, probably either 'Psyche' or 'Cinch.'"

* * * * *

A clergyman was on board a steamer which was caught in a severe gale. The rolling was constant and seemed to get worse as time went on. At last the good man got thoroughly frightened. He believed they were destined for a watery grave, so he went to the captain and asked if he might have prayers. The captain took him by the arm and led him to the forecastle, where the tars were singing and swearing. "There," said he, "when you hear the men swearing you may know there is no danger." The clergyman went back feeling better, but still the storm increased and his alarm also. Disconsolate, he managed to stagger to the forecastle again, where he heard the sailors swearing as hard as ever. "Mary," he said to his sympathetic wife as he crawled back to his berth, "Mary, thank God, they're swearing yet."

* * * * *

"Hawaiian servants," said a woman with some experience of them, "are the best in the world, but they are strangely unsophisticated, strangely naive. They insist on calling you by your first name. Ours were always saying to my husband, 'Yes, John,' or 'all right, John,' and to me 'very well, Ann,' or 'Ann, I am going out.' At last I got tired of this and to John, when we got a new cook, I said: Don't ever call me by my first name in the cook's presence. Then, perhaps, not knowing my name, he'll have to say 'Mrs.' to me. So John was careful to address me as 'dearie,' or 'sweetheart,' the watchful chap gave me no title at all. One day we had some

English officers to dine. I told them how I had overcome, in my new cook's case, the native servants' abuse of their employer's Christian names, and I said, By this servant, at least, you won't hear me called 'Ann.'" Just then the new cook entered the room. He bowed to me respectfully and said:

"'Sweetheart, dinner is served!'

"'What?' I stammered.

"'Dinner is served, dearie!' answered the cook."

* * * * *

Early one morning, on the second day out, a terribly seasick passenger, pale and hollow-eyed, came out of his stateroom and ran into a lady, who was coming along the passageway, clad in the scantiest raiment. She screamed and started to run. "Don't be alarmed," groaned the man. "Don't be alarmed, madam; I shall never live to tell it."

* * * * *

Mike and Pat worked for a wealthy farmer. They planned to turn burglars and steal the money which the farmer had hid in one of the rooms of his house. They waited until midnight, then started to do the job.

In order to get the money they had to pass the farmer's bedroom. Mike said, "I'll go first, and if it's all right you can follow and do just the same as I."

Mike started to pass the room. Just as he got opposite the door the floor creaked. This awoke the farmer, who called out, "Who's there?"

Mike answered with a "meaow!" (imitating a cat). The farmer's wife being awake, too, said, "Oh, John, it's the cat," and all was quiet.

Now Pat started to pass the door, and as he got opposite it the floor creaked again. The farmer called out again, louder than before, "Who's there?"

Pat answered, "Another cat."

* * * * *

Softleigh—"Good evening, Mrs. Moran. I came to see if your daughter, Miss Mabel, would go for a walk with me."

Miss Mabel—"How do you do, Mr. Softleigh? I shall be delighted. Mama, do I look fit to go to a restaurant?"

* * * * *

They were on their honeymoon. He had bought a catboat and had taken her out to show her how well he could handle a boat, putting her to tend the sheet. A puff of wind came, and he shouted in no uncertain tones, "Let go the sheet." No response. Then again, "Let go that sheet, quick." Still no movement. A few minutes later, when both were clinging to the bottom of the overturned boat, he said:

"Why didn't you let go that sheet when I told you to, dear?"

"I would have," said the bride, "if you had not been so rough about it. You ought to speak more kindly to your wife."

* * * * *

Madam—"Put plenty of nuts in the cake."

Cook—"I'll crack no more nuts to-day, me jaw hurts me already."

* * * * *

Mother—"Alice, it is bedtime. All the little chickens have gone to bed."

Alice—"Yes, mama, and so has the hen."

* * * * *

Few men have ever been so ready and witty as Mark Twain in introducing others to public audiences. At Hartford, December 12, 1877, he presented Mr. Howells, and, after a word or two as to his literary work, said, "But I am not here to speak of his literary reputation, but simply to (a long pause) back up his moral character."

* * * * *

A Lancashire vicar was asked by the choir to call upon old Betty, who was deaf, but who insisted in joining in the solo of the anthem, and to ask her only to sing in the hymns. He shouted into her ear: "Betty! I've been requested to speak to you about your singing." At last she caught the word "singing," and replied: "Not to me be the praise, sir; it's a gift."

* * * * *

The proprietor of a large drug store recently received this curt and haughty note written in an angular, feminine hand: "I do not want vasioline, but glisserine. Is that plain enough? I persoom you can spell."

* * * * *

It was in a Maine Sunday-school that a teacher recently asked a Chinese pupil she was teaching to read if he understood the meaning of the words "an old cow."

"Been cow a long time," was the prompt answer.

* * * * *

Upon moving into a new neighborhood the small boy of the family was cautioned not to fight with his new acquaintances. One day Willie came home with a black eye and very much spattered with dirt.

"Why, Willie," said mama, "I thought I told you to count a hundred before you fought!"

"I did, mama," said Willie, "and look what Tommy Smith did while I was counting!"

* * * * *

"The rolling stone gathers no moss," quoted the man who had never been outside his home county.

"True," rejoined the globe-trotter, "but it acquires an enviable polish."

* * * * *

Curate (who is going to describe his little holiday in Lucerne)—"My dear friends—I will not call you ladies and gentlemen, since I know you too well."

* * * * *

Daniel Purcell, the famous punster, was desired to make a pun extempore.

"Upon what subject?" said Daniel.

"The king," answered the other.

"Oh! sir," said he "the king is no subject."

* * * * *

Illustrative of "that troublesome Henglish haitch" an American traveler relates the following:

Once I dined with an English farmer. We had ham—very delicious baked ham. The farmer's son soon finished his portion and passed his plate again.

"More 'am, father," he said.

The farmer frowned.

"Don't say 'am, son. Say *'am.*"

"I did say 'am," the lad protested in an injured tone.

"You said *'am,*" cried the father fiercely. "'Am's what it should be. 'Am, not 'am."

In the middle of the squabble the farmer's wife turned to me and, with a deprecatory little laugh, explained:

"They both think they're sayin' 'am, sir."

* * * * *

Passing along Princes Street, Edinburgh, one day a herculean Scots Grey stopped at the post-office and called on a street arab to polish his boots. The feet of the dragoon were in proportion to his height and, looking at the tremendous boots before him, the arab knelt down on the pavement and shouted out to his chum across the road, "Jamie, come ower an' gie's a hand, I've got an army contract."

* * * * *

The younger man had been complaining that he could not get his wife to mend his clothes.

"I asked her to sew a button on this vest last night, and she hasn't touched it," he said. At this the older man assumed the air of a patriarch.

"Never ask a woman to mend anything," he said. "You haven't been married very long, and I think I can give you some serviceable suggestions. When I want a shirt mended I take it to my wife, flourish it around a little and say, 'Where's that rag-bag?'

"'What do you want of the rag-bag?' asks my wife. Her suspicions are roused at once.

"'I want to throw this shirt away; it's worn out,' I say, with a few more flourishes.

"'Let me see that shirt,' my wife says then. 'Now, John, hand it to me at once.'

"Of course, I pass it over, and she examines it. 'Why, John Taylor,' she is sure to say, 'I never knew such extravagance! This is a perfectly good shirt. All it needs is— —' And then she mends it."

* * * * *

A browbeating counsel asked a witness how far he had been from a certain place. "Just four yards, two feet, and six inches," was the reply. "How come you to be so exact, my friend?" "I expected some fool or other would ask me, so I measured it."

* * * * *

"Now, see here, porter," said the drummer briskly, "I want you to put me off at Syracuse. You know we get in there about six o'clock in the morning, and I may over-sleep myself. But it is important that I should get out. Here's a five-dollar gold piece. Now, I may wake up hard. Don't mind if I kick. Pay no attention if I'm ugly. I want you to put me off the train no matter how hard I fight. Understand?"

"Yes, sah," answered the sturdy Nubian. "It shall be did, sah!"

The next morning the coin-giver was awakened by a stentorian voice calling: "Rochester!"

"Rochester!" he exclaimed, sitting up. "Where's that porter?"

Hastily slipping on his trousers, he went in search of the negro, and found him in the porter's closet, huddled up, with his head in a bandage, his clothes torn, and his arm in a sling.

"Well," said the drummer, "you are a sight. Why didn't you put me off at Syracuse?"

"Wha-at!" gasped the porter, jumping up, as his eyes bulged from his head. "Was you de gemman dat give me a five-dollah gold piece?"

"Of course I was, you idiot!"

"Well, den, befoah de Lawd, who was dat gemman I put off at Syracuse?"

* * * * *

A right reverend prelate, himself a man of extreme good-nature, was frequently much vexed in spirit by the proud, froward, perverse, and untractable temper of his next vicar. The latter, after an absence much longer than usual, one day paid a visit to the bishop, who kindly inquired the cause of his absence, and was answered by the vicar that he had been confined to his house for some time past by an obstinate stiffness in his knee. "I am glad of that," replied the prelate; "'tis a good symptom that the disorder has changed place, for I had a long time thought it immovably settled in your neck."

* * * * *

Bride—"George, dear, when we reach our destination let us try to avoid giving the impression that we are newly married."

George—"All right, Maud; you can carry the suitcase and umbrellas."

* * * * *

Francis Wilson was speaking at the Players Club of New York City, not long ago, of the all too prevalent ignorance of dramatic literature in the country to-day.

"Why," said Mr. Wilson, "a company was playing 'She Stoops to Conquer' in a small Western town last winter when a man without any money, wishing to see the show, stepped up to the box office and said:

"'Pass me in, please.'

"The box office man gave a loud, harsh laugh.

"'Pass you in? What for?' he asked.

"The applicant drew himself up and answered, haughtily: 'What for? Why, because I am Oliver Goldsmith, author of the play.'

"'Oh, I beg your pardon, sir,' replied the other in a meek voice, as he hurriedly wrote an order for a box."

* * * * *

Lady Bountiful—"All I can say is, Jenkins, that if these people insist on building these horrid little villas near my gates, I shall leave the place."

Jenkins—"Exactly what I told them at the meeting, your ladyship. I said, 'Do you want to drive away the goose that lays the golden eggs?'"

* * * * *

Old Lady (to conductor—her first drive on an electric tram).—"Would it be dangerous, conductor, if I was to put my foot on the rail?"

Conductor (an Edison manqué).—"No, mum, not unless you was to put the other one on the overhead wire!"

* * * * *

After a few weeks at boarding-school Alice wrote home as follows:

> *"Dear Father*—Though I was homesick at first, now that I am getting acquainted, I like the school very much. Last evening Grayce and Kathryn (my roommates) and I had a nice little chafing-dish party, and we invited three other girls, Mayme and Carrye Miller and Edyth Kent. I hope you are all well at home. I can't write any more now for I have a lot of studying to do. With lots of love to all.
>
> "Your affectionate daughter,
> "ALYSS."

To this she received the following reply:

> *"My dear Daughter Alyss*—I was glad to receive your letter and to know that you are enjoying yourself. Uncle Jaymes came the other day, bringing Charls and Albyrt with him. Your brother Henrie was delighted, for he has been lonely without you. I have bought a new gray horse whose name is Byllye. He matches nicely with old Fredde. With much love from us all, I am,
>
> > "Your affectionate father,
> > "WYLLYAM JONES."

The next letter from the absent daughter was signed "Alice."

* * * * *

While Chauncey M. Depew was at the Omaha Exposition, he and President Callaway of the New York Central chanced to go into a booth on the Midway Plaisance.

It was a tame entertainment and there was only a meager attendance when Mr. Depew and Mr. Callaway entered. Their stay would have been very brief except for the fact that they had scarcely taken their seats before there began a steady inpouring of people, which continued until the small auditorium was crowded.

Taking this extraordinary increase of spectators as an indication that something of an interesting nature was about to be disclosed, the two New Yorkers concluded to sit it out. Half an hour's waiting failed to reward their patient expectancy, however, and Mr. Callaway suggested that they move on.

Just then ex-Secretary of Agriculture J. Sterling Morton pushed his way through the crowd, and, extending his hand to Mr. Depew, exclaimed:

"Well, Doctor Depew, so you are really here! I thought that 'barker' was lying."

"What do you mean?" inquired Mr. Depew.

"Why, the 'barker' for this show is standing outside and inviting the crowd to 'step up lively' and pay ten cents for the privilege of seeing the 'great and only Chauncey M. Depew.'"

* * * * *

That the royal road to learning is full of strange pitfalls is shown by some of the definitions and statements given by school-children—some of whom are well along the way. The following are *bona fide* samples coming under the knowledge of one teacher:

"About this time Columbus was cursing around among the West Indies."

"Jackson's campaign in the Valley was the greatest piece of millinery-work ever known."

"The Valkyrie were the Choosers of the Slain, and the Valhalla the Haulers of the Slain."

"The eldest son of the King of France is called The Dolphin."

"The Duke of Clarence, according to his usual custom, was killed in battle."

"Heathen are paragons (pagans) that wash up idle things."

"The Indians call their women squabs."

* * * * *

A certain curate in the course of conversation at a dinner party some time ago remarked to a friend, "I had a curious dream last night, but as it was about my vicar I hardly like to tell it." On being pressed, however, he began: "I dreamt I was dead and was on my way to Heaven, which was reached by a very long ladder. At the foot I was met by an angel, who pressed a piece of chalk into my hand and said, 'If you climb long enough you will reach Heaven, but for every sin you are conscious of having committed you must mark a rung of the ladder with the chalk as you go up.' I took the chalk and started. I had climbed up very, very far and was feeling very tired when I suddenly met my vicar coming down. 'Hullo!' I said, 'what are you going down for?' 'More chalk.'"

* * * * *

Mrs. McKinley used to tell of a colored widow whose children she had helped educate. The widow, rather late in life, married.

"How are you getting on?" Mrs. McKinley asked her a few months after her marriage.

"Fine, thank yo', ma'am," the bride answered.

"And is your husband a good provider?"

"'Deed he am a good providah, ma'am," was the enthusiastic reply. "Why, jes' dis las' week he got me five new places to wash at."

* * * * *

A certain curate was of a painfully nervous temperament, and in consequence was constantly making awkward remarks—intended as compliments—to the bishop and others. Having distinguished himself in an unusual degree during a gathering of clergy to an afternoon tea at the bishop's palace, he was taken to task for his failings by a senior curate, who was one of his companions on the way home.

"Look here, Bruce," said the senior decidedly, "you are a donkey! Why can not you keep quiet, instead of making your asinine remarks? I am speaking to you now as a brother— —"

Loud laughter interrupted him at this point, and for the moment he wondered why.

* * * * *

An earnest clergyman one Sunday morning was exhorting those who had anxious and troubled consciences to be sure and call on their pastor for guidance and prayer.

"To show you, my brethren, the blessed results of these visits with your pastor," said he, "I will state to you that only yesterday a gentleman of wealth called upon me for counsel and instruction; and now to-day, my friends—to-day he sits among us, not only a Christian, but a happy husband and father."

A young lady in the audience whispered to a matron: "Wasn't that pretty quick work?"

* * * * *

A good story is told of the late George Augustus Sala in his early and impecunious days. At some festive gathering where Mr. Sala was present, Mr. Attemborough, the famous pawnbroker, was also a guest. They recognized each other, and shook hands.

"How do you do, Mr. Attemborough," said the journalist. "We have met often before, but I think this is the first time I have ever seen your legs."

* * * * *

A clergyman in the West Country had two curates, one a comparatively old man, the other very young. With the former he had not been able to work agreeably; and on being invited to another living, he accepted it, and took the young curate with him. Naturally, there was a farewell sermon; and we can imagine the feelings of the curate who was to be left behind when he heard the text given out, "Abide ye here with the ass, and I and the lad will go yonder and worship."

* * * * *

A bishop was staying with a friend in a country house. On Sunday morning as he passed through the library he found a small boy curled up in a big chair, deeply interested in a book.

"Are you going to church, Tom?" he asked.

"No, sir," he replied.

"Why, I am," said the Bishop.

"Huh," said the boy, "you've got to go. It's your job."

* * * * *

A celebrated continental specialist to whom time was literally money and who was possessed of a fiery temper made it a rule that all patients should undress before entering his consulting room so as not to waste any of his valuable time. One day a meek-looking little man entered with all his clothes on. "What do you mean by coming in like that?" said the doctor in a rage. "Go and strip at once!" "But I—" faltered the man. "I tell you I've no time to waste," yelled the doctor, and the poor man left the room in haste. When his turn came he reentered the room. "Now then," said the doctor, "that's better. What can I do for you?" "I called to collect your subscription for the benevolent society."

* * * * *

A tall man, impatiently pacing the platform of a wayside station, accosted a red-haired boy of about twelve.

"S-s-say," he said, "d-d-do y-you know ha-ha-how late this train is?"

The boy grinned but made no reply. The man stuttered out something about red-headed kids in general and passed into the station.

A stranger, overhearing the one-sided conversation, asked the boy why he hadn't answered the big man.

"D-d-d'ye wanter see me g-g-get me fa-fa-face punched?" stammered the boy. "D-d-dat big g-g-guy'd tink I was mo-mo-mocking him."

* * * * *

"Mother," said a college student who had brought his chum home for the holidays, "permit me to present my friend, Mr. Specknoodle."

His mother, who was a little hard of hearing, placed her hand to her ear.

"I'm sorry, George, but I didn't quite catch your friend's name. You'll have to speak a little louder, I'm afraid."

"I say, mother," shouted George, "I want to present my friend Mr. *Specknoo-dle.*"

"I'm sorry, George, but Mr. —— What was the name again?"

"Mr. SPECKNOODLE!" George fairly yelled.

The old lady shook her head sadly.

"I'm sorry, George, but I'm afraid it's no use. It sounds just like Specknoodle to me."

* * * * *

A young American lady on a visit to London was being shown some of the sights by a boastful Englishman. "This is a cannon captured at Bunker Hill," said the Englishman. "How interesting," exclaimed the lady. "I must explain," said the gentleman tauntingly, "that this cannon was captured from the Americans by the English." The lady quietly retorted, "Well, you have the cannon; we have the hill."

* * * * *

Former Congressman Fred Landis of Indiana has made a reputation for himself as an orator. A year or so ago Landis, speaking at the unveiling of a monument to President Lincoln, uttered the phrase, "Abraham Lincoln—that mystic mingling of star and clod." This was loudly applauded. After the speech a friend of Landis approached him, and, repeating the phrase, said: "Fred, what in the name of heaven does that mean?" Putting his arm around his friend's shoulder, Landis replied: "I don't know, really, but it gets 'em every time."

* * * * *

Captain Foretopp tells a story of a certain noted divine who was on his steamer when a great gale overtook them off the Oregon coast. "It looks pretty bad," said the Bishop to the Captain. "Couldn't be much worse, Bishop," replied Foretopp.

Half an hour later the steamer was diving under the waves as if she were a submarine and leaking like an old door. "Looks worse, I think, Captain," said the Bishop. "We must trust in Providence now, Bishop," answered Foretopp.

"Oh, I hope it has not come to that," gasped the Bishop.

* * * * *

A couple of New Yorkers were playing golf on a New Jersey course on Election Day when they saw a fine-appearing old gentleman looking at them wistfully. They asked him to join the game, which he did with alacrity. He was mild in speech and manner and played well. But once when he had made a foozle he ejaculated vehemently the word: "Croton!" A few minutes later when he made another bad play, he repeated: "Croton!" The third time he said it, one of his new-made friends said: "I don't want to be inquisitive, but will you tell me why you say 'Croton' so often?" "Well," said the old gentleman, "isn't that the biggest dam near New York?" He was a Presbyterian clergyman from Brooklyn.

* * * * *

Willie, aged five, was taken by his father to his first football game. The feature that caught his chief approval, however, did not become evident until he said his prayers that night. To the horror of his parents Willie prayed with true football snap:

"God bless papa,
God bless mama,
God bless Willie;
Rah! Rah! Rah!"

* * * * *

A suburban minister during his discourse one Sabbath morning said: "In each blade of grass there is a sermon." The following day one of his flock discovered the good man pushing a lawn mower about his garden and paused to say: "Well, parson, I'm glad to see you engaged in cutting your sermons short."

* * * * *

"Now, Bobby," instructed the Fond Maternal Parent of the prodigy in velveteens, bound for a children's party, "the weather looks rather threatening. Here is half a dollar for you, and if it rains come back by cab."

Two hours later it came down cats and dogs, and F. M. P. (Fond Maternal Parent) returned devout thanks for her forethought.

But when little Bobby Velveteens returned he was wet to the skin.

"Why, Bobby," cried the F. M. P., "didn't you come back by cab, as I told you?"

"Oh, yes, ma!" answered Bobby. "And it was simply splendid! I rode on the box beside the driver!"

* * * * *

A Bishop of the Episcopal Church lived all his life unwed. A friend mentioned that one of the States was imposing a tax on bachelors, to be increased a certain percentage every ten years of bachelorhood, and added: "Why, Bishop, at your age you would have to pay a hundred dollars a year."

"Well," said the Bishop quietly, "it's worth it."

* * * * *

Two old women, on their way home from church, in a country district of Scotland, were speaking of Napoleon's overthrow, by the allied troops at Waterloo. The minister had been pointing a moral by aid of the Corsican hero's defeat.

"Hoo is it," said one, in her narrow way, "the Scotch aye win their battles?"

"Weel, ye ken, it's because they aye pray afore they go in the fecht," replied the other.

"Ay! But mercy, wuman, canna the French pray, as weel?"

"Nae doobt, they dae; but wha could understan' they jabberin' bodies?" snapped the interrogated one, in peremptory answer.

* * * * *

Curiously worded advertisements that are funny without intent are common in the London papers. Here are a few examples:

"A boy wanted who can open oysters with references."

"Bulldog for sale; will eat anything, very fond of children."

"Wanted an organist and a boy to blow the same."

"Wanted, a boy to be partly outside and partly inside the counter."

"Lost, near Highgate Archway, an umbrella belonging to a gentleman with a bent rib and a bone handle."

"To be disposed of, a mail phaeton, the property of a gentleman with a movable headpiece as good as new."

* * * * *

A tall young man stalked with stately stride into the office of a small hotel in a remote part of the White Mountains. Behind him came a severe valet carrying bags and a gun-case, and on a wagon at the door were two prosperous trunks. In an armchair behind the hotel counter sat a spare old man placidly chewing tobacco and reading the "Weekly Recorder."

"Ah-h-h! Hm!" the tall young man began. "Is this Mr. Silas P. Meacham, proprietor of this hotel?"

"Yaas," replied the old one, glancing up over his paper.

"I am Mr. Hanningford Wattster van Derventer, of the Metropolis Club, of New York," said the visitor, impressively. "My friend, Mr. Vandergilt, told me you would take excellent care of me here."

"Ya-as," replied Silas, still buried in his paper.

"*I* am Mr. Hanningford Wattster van Derventer, of New York," the visitor repeated. "My friend, Mr. Vandergilt, told me you would take excellent care of me here."

"Ya-a-as," said Silas, still chewing and reading his paper.

"*I* am Mr. Hanningford Wattster van Derventer, of New York," the young man reiterated with the air of one who tells great news, also with rising indignation. "My friend, Mr. *Vandergilt*, told me you would take excellent care of me—show me every attention."

"Wa-al," exclaimed Silas P. Meacham, throwing down the paper and revealing his few yellow teeth in a mocking grin—"wa-al, what d'ye want me t' do—kiss ye?"

* * * * *

Court—(to prosecutor)—"Then you recognize this handkerchief as the one which was stolen?"

Prosecutor—"Yes, your honor."

Court—"And yet it isn't the only handkerchief of the sort in the world. See, this one I have in my pocket is exactly like it."

Prosecutor—"Very likely, your honor; there were two stolen."

* * * * *

The company of soldiers had been receiving a lesson in minor tactics, and among other subjects was the method of patrols in getting information. The book said that information could be obtained from "mayors, postmasters, livery-stable keepers, doctors, peasants, etc."

The lieutenant turned to Finnegan and said: "Do you know what a peasant is, Finnegan?"

He answered promptly, "Yes, sor."

"Well, what is it?"

"It's a bird, sor," said Finnegan with evident pride.

* * * * *

Senator Pettus, of Alabama, was writing with a noisy, spluttering pen. Laying it down, he smiled and said: "Once I was spending the evening with a friend of mine in Selma. We sat in the dining-room and from the kitchen came a dreadful scratching sound. 'Martha,' said my friend to the maid, 'what is that scratching? it must be the dog trying to get in.' 'Huh!' said Martha, 'Dat ain' no dog, dat's cook writin' a love-letter to heh honeysuckle.'"

* * * * *

"No smoking in this coach, sir," said the conductor of a passenger train. "I'm not smokin'," answered the passenger with an injured air from the depths of his seat.

"You've got your pipe in your mouth," declared the conductor with emphasis, sharply confident. "I hov," retorted the Hibernian, "and I hov me fut in me shoe, too, but I'm not walkin'."

* * * * *

Little Alice is old for her years. One evening after she had gone to bed she heard mama and papa laughing in much enjoyment over a game of flinch; she longed to get up and join them, but knew she must not. The next morning at breakfast she was very quiet. Presently she drew a deep sigh, and said, "What a good time you and papa had last night. Oh, I feel the need of a husband, mama, I *do* feel it!"

* * * * *

A teacher in one of the primary schools of New York recently read to her pupils "The Old Oaken Bucket."

After explaining the song to them very carefully, she asked the class to copy the first stanza from the blackboard, where she had written it, and try to illustrate the verse by drawings in the same way a story is illustrated.

In a short while one little girl handed up her paper with several little dots between two lines, a circle, half a dozen dots, and three buckets.

"I do not quite understand this, Mamie," said the teacher, kindly. "What is that circle?"

"Oh, that's the well," Mamie replied.

"And why do you have three buckets?" again asked the teacher.

"One," answered the child, "is the oaken bucket, one is the iron-bound bucket, and the other is the moss-covered bucket that hung in the well."

"But, Mamie, what are all these little dots for?"

"Why those are the spots which my infancy knew," earnestly replied Mamie.

* * * * *

Four gentlemen went out to dine. They were Arthur Balfour, Joseph Chamberlain, Lord Charles Beresford, and the Japanese Minister. Mr. Arthur Balfour was standing treat and said to Joey, "What will you take?" "Oh, thanks, I'll take Scotch, Arthur." "And what will you take, Lord Charles?" "Oh, thanks, I'll take Irish, Arthur." "And now, what will you take?" addressing the Japanese Minister. "I'll take Port Arthur, thanks."

* * * * *

Not long after the great Chelsea fire some children in Newton, Massachusetts, held a Charity Fair by which eighteen dollars were realized. This they forwarded to the rector of a certain Boston church who had taken a prominent part in the relief work, with a letter which read somewhat as follows:

> "We have had a fair and made eighteen dollars. We are sending it to you. Please give it to the Chelsea sufferers.

"Yours truly, etc.

"P. S. We hope the suffering is not all over."

* * * * *

A story is told of a certain committee meeting in which the proceedings commenced with noise and gradually became uproarious. At last one of the disputants, losing all control over his emotions, exclaimed to his opponent: "Sir, you are, I think, the biggest ass that I ever had the misfortune to set eyes upon!" "Order! order!" said the chairman, gravely; "you seem to forget that I am in the room."

* * * * *

An Irish priest had labored hard with one of his flock to induce him to give up whisky. "I tell you, Michael," said the priest, "whisky is your worst enemy, and you should keep as far away from it as you can." "The enemy is it, father?" responded Michael, "and it was your riverence's self that was telling us in the pulpit last Sunday to love our enemies." "So I was, Michael," rejoined the priest, "but I didn't tell you to swallow them."

* * * * *

A Sabbath-school worker was visiting a Sabbath-school some distance from home. Being called upon to address the school, he commenced by asking, "Who can tell me something about Peter?" (the lesson was about Peter that day). Having received no answer from either large or small pupils, he again made the request. This time a little girl put up her hand. He called the little girl to him and placed her upon a chair. After complimenting her on her bravery and brightness, he asked her to tell him all she knew about Peter. In return came the following:

> "Peter, Peter, pumpkin-eater,
> Had a wife and couldn't keep her;
> Put her in a pumpkin shell
> Where he kept her very well."

* * * * *

Senator Beveridge, in recommending broad and generous views to the graduating class of a medical school, told this story:

"I once saw two famous physicians introduced at a reception. They were deservedly famous, but they were of opposing schools; and the regular, as he shook the other by the hand, said loudly:

"'I am glad to meet you as a gentleman, sir, though I can't admit that you are a physician.'

"'And I,' said the homeopathist, smiling faintly, 'am glad to meet you as a physician, though I can't admit you are a gentleman.'"

* * * * *

At a recent dinner in London the conversation turned to the subject of lynching in the United States. It was the general opinion that a large percentage of Americans met death at the end of a rope. Finally the hostess turned to an American, who had taken no part in the conversation, and said:

"You, sir, must have often seen these affairs."

"Yes," he replied, "we take a kind of municipal pride in seeing which city can show the greatest number of lynchings yearly."

"Oh, do tell us about a lynching you have seen yourself," broke in half a dozen voices at once.

"The night before I sailed for England," said Eugene Field, "I was giving a dinner at a hotel to a party of intimate friends when a colored waiter spilled a plate of soup over the gown of a lady at an adjoining table. The gown was utterly ruined, and the gentlemen of her party at once seized the waiter, tied a rope around his neck, and at a signal from the injured lady swung him into the air."

"Horrible," said the hostess with a shudder. "And did you actually see this yourself?"

"Well, no," admitted the American apologetically. "Just at that moment I happened to be downstairs killing the chef for putting mustard in the blanc mange."

* * * * *

Mrs. Jones recently spent a few days at a farm, and in a moment of originality bought some poultry from the farmer with a view to their providing fresh eggs for breakfast every morning. She sent them to town per the local carrier, despatching a note at the same time to her husband telling him to look out for the consignment. When Jones reached home from his office he inquired if the poultry had arrived. The servant told him they had, but the man had carelessly put them in the back yard, leaving the door open, and they had all escaped. Thereupon a fowl hunt was immediately organized. The next day Jones saw the carrier. "Nice trick you played me yesterday," said he; "spent three hours hunting those fowls and only found ten." "Then think yourself blessed lucky," replied the man. "I only brought six."

* * * * *

A patronizing young lord was seated opposite the late James McNeill Whistler at dinner one evening. During a lull in the conversation he adjusted his monocle and leaned forward toward the artist.

"Aw, y' know, Mr. Whistler," he drawled, "I pahssed your house this mawning."

"Thank you," said Whistler quietly. "Thank you very much."

* * * * *

The new minister in a Georgia church was delivering his first sermon. The darky janitor was a critical listener from a back corner of the church. The minister's sermon was eloquent, and his prayers seemed to cover the whole category of human wants.

After the services one of the deacons asked the old darky what he thought of the new minister. "Don't you think he offers up a good prayer, Joe?"

"Ah mos' suhtainly does, boss. Why, dat man axed de good Lord fo' things dat de odder preacher didn't even know He had!"

* * * * *

For weeks the kindergarten had been deluged with nature verses, and the process of absorption was far advanced. Sufficiently to admit of a little squeezing with results, thought the teacher.

"Now, children," she said, "I want you each to bring in a little verse that you have made yourselves about the buds, or the trees, or the flowers, or anything that pleases you."

Various specimens were produced next day, but the gem of the collection was little May Flynn's. With appropriate gestures she recited:

> "See the pretty gold fish swimming in the globe!
> See the pretty robin singing in the tree!
> Who teached these two to fly together?
> Who stucked the fur upon their breasts?
> 'Twas God. 'Twas God. He done it."

* * * * *

A story about King Edward is worth repeating. Just before the illness which caused the postponement of the coronation, he was racing down one of the country roads in his motor-car at a speed which was away beyond the legal limit.

"Hi! Hi!" called a policeman. "Stop there, in the name of the law!"

His Majesty is said to have slackened speed and called out: "But I'm the king!"

"Jest you come aht o' that," was the reply; "yer the third king wot's come along this morning."

* * * * *

In order to play "Rosemary" some years ago, John Drew shaved off his mustache, thereby greatly changing his appearance. Shortly afterward he met Max Beerbohm in the lobby of a London theater, but could not just then recall who the latter was. Mr. Beerbohm's memory was better.

"Oh, Mr. Drew," he said, "I'm afraid you don't know me without your mustache."

* * * * *

A truly eloquent parson had been preaching for an hour or so on the immortality of the soul.

"I looked at the mountains," he declaimed, "and could not help thinking, 'Beautiful as you are, you will be destroyed, while my soul will not.' I gazed upon the ocean and cried, 'Mighty as you are you will eventually dry up, but not I.'"

* * * * *

"Now if I don't git rid o' dis cold soon," complained Jimmy, the jockey, "I'll be a dead one."

"Did you go to Dr. Goodman, as I told you?" asked his friend.

"Naw! De sign on his door said '10 to 1' an' I wouldn't monkey wid no long shot like dat."

* * * * *

Herbert S. Stone, the publisher, described at a dinner in Washington the amusing methods of a newspaper writer who used to write articles at a set rate a column.

He was once commissioned to do a serial story for a Chicago paper. The story, as it proceeded from week to week, was interesting, but it contained many passages like the following:

"Did you hear him?"

"I did."

"Truly?"

"Truly."

"Where?"

"By the well."

"When?"

"To-day."

"Then he lives?"

"He does."

"Ah."

The editor, sending for the man, said:

"Hereafter we will pay you by the letters in your serial. We will pay you so much a thousand letters."

The young man, looking crestfallen, went away, but in the very next instalment of his story he introduced a character who stuttered, and all through the chapter were scattered passages like this:

"B-b-b-b-believe me, s-s-s-sir, I am n-n-not g-g-g-guilty. M-m-m-my m-m-m-mother c-c-c-committed this c-c-c-crime."

* * * * *

A man with a soft, low voice had just completed his purchases in a department store of the City of Churches.

"What is the name?" asked the clerk.

"Jepson," replied the man.

"Chipson?"

"No, Jepson."

"Oh, yes, Jefferson."

"No, Jepson; J-e-p-s-o-n."

"Jepson?"

"That's it. You have it. Sixteen eighty-two—"

"Your first name, initial, please."

"Oh, K."

"O. K. Jepson."

"Excuse me, it isn't O. K. You did not understand me. I said 'Oh.'"

"O. Jepson."

"No; rub out the O and let the K stand."

The clerk looked annoyed. "Will you please give me your initials again?"

"I said K."

"I beg your pardon, you said O. K. Perhaps you had better write it yourself."

"I said 'Oh'—"

"Just now you said K."

"Allow me to finish what I started to say. I said 'Oh,' because I did not understand what you were asking me. I did not mean that it was my initial. My name is Kirby Jepson."

"Oh!"

"No, not O., but K.," said the man. "Give me the pencil, and I'll write it down for you myself. There, I guess it's O. K. now."

* * * * *

The furnishing of the new house had gone on vociferously. All the family told stories of the beautiful and rare articles picked up at auctions, usually at such bargains as only amateurs in such matters are able to find. There was naturally much curiosity to see how the house looked. The first visitor who had the opportunity to inspect it was eagerly questioned by her friends.

"I can't describe it myself," she explained. "All I can say is that auctions speak louder than words."

* * * * *

When Frank R. Stockton started out with his Rudder Grange experiences he undertook to keep chickens. One old motherly Plymouth Rock brought out a brood late in the fall, and Stockton named each of the chicks after some literary friend, among the rest Mary Mapes Dodge. Mrs. Dodge was visiting the farm some time later, and, happening to think of her namesake, she said: "By the way, Frank, how does little Mary Mapes Dodge get along?" "The funny thing about little Mary Mapes Dodge," said he, "is, she turns out to be Thomas Bailey Aldrich."

* * * * *

A short time ago a lady with an only child (aged seven) was entertaining the bishop of the diocese to afternoon tea. The small girl was allowed to come to tea, but her mother had instilled into her mind the necessity of speaking reverently to the bishop. Tea came and with it the pangs of hunger, but at the same time her mother's warning, "speak reverently," was always before her. After sitting for about ten minutes gazing at the good things and repeating over and over again, "speak reverently," she exclaimed, "For God's sake pass me the bread and butter."

* * * * *

Hiram Hardscrabble and his load of hay, two horses, and a perfectly good wagon were pitched so high and so far by a reckless railroad train that when they came down they weren't—any of 'em—good for much. The local Congressman took the case, and after some months advised Hiram to accept the railroad company's offer of lifelong employment at $15 a week. Hiram accepted. They put him out as a flagman on a crossing near his native village.

Cassidy, the section boss, stopped his handcar before the flag-shanty, and after a searching look at Hiram advised as follows:

"So you're the new flagman, are ye? And ye've niver railroaded before. No harm. We'll make a man iv ye. See, now, there's yer red flag and yer green flag and yer white flag, and yer thrain schedule within on the wall. All ye have to do is dhrop the gates befoor the thrains do come, so that they'll have a clear thrack. D'ye mind, now?

"But there's wan thing above all others—th' Impire Shtate Express! Putt yer gates down two minyits before she comes and keep them down till she's pasht. Mind now, she must niver be late on this section. Niver wan minyit late. I won't sthand f'r it. Remimber—th' Impire Shtate Express. She must niver be late here."

Hiram promised. At 2 P.M., when the Empire State Express was due in two minutes, he dropped the crossing gates and stood by with the white flag to wave her along. Three minutes passed, four, five—and still no train. As a matter of fact, she had lost half an hour at an open draw on the Harlem River in the morning, and was laboring mightily to regain lost time in spite of her fast schedule.

Seven minutes late, and then Hiram heard a wild shriek a mile away and saw the express coming. He darted into the shanty, grabbed a red flag, and leaped out upon the track, waving it furiously. The engineer shut off, threw over the reverse lever, gave her sand and the air; and the mighty train stopped short, in a whirl of sand, cinders, and sparks, brakes creaking and passengers pitchpoling everywhere.

"What's the matter now?" roared the engineer, thrusting half his body out of the cab and glaring down at Hiram.

"Be yeou th' ingineer?" asked the flagman, peering at him with suspicion.

"Yes, yes! Whad-do-you want?"

"I want t' know whut's made ye so goldinged late? Cassidy says he wun't stand f'r it."

* * * * *

During a match at St. Andrews, Scotland, a rustic was struck in the eye accidentally by a golf ball. Running up to his assailant, he yelled:

"This'll cost ye five pounds—five pounds!"

"But I called out 'fore' as loudly as I could," explained the golfer.

"Did ye, sir?" replied the troubled one, much appeased. "Weel, I didna hear; I'll take fower."

* * * * *

Mark Twain observed once at a public dinner that he had written a friendly letter to Queen Victoria protesting against a tax being levied in England on his head, on the ground that it was a gas-works. "I don't know you," he wrote, "but I've met your son. He was at the head of a procession in the Strand, and I was on a 'bus." Years afterward he met the King at Homburg, and they had a long talk. At parting the King said: "I am glad to have met you again." That last word troubled Mark, who asked whether the King had not mistaken him for some one else. The reply—"Why, don't you remember meeting me in the Strand when I was at the head of a procession and you were on a 'bus?" revealed the strength of Royal memories.

* * * * *

An Irishman and an Englishman were recounting feats of physical prowess. The Englishman, by way of showing his strength, said that he was accustomed to swim across the Thames three times before breakfast every morning.

"Well," said the Irishman, "that may be all right, but it do seem to me that your clothes would be on the wrong side of the river all the time."

* * * * *

An excess luggage porter at a large railway station said to a "commercial," "I see your luggage is overweight, sir." "Ah! your visionary powers are far too acute for me, my friend." "What did you say, sir?" "I say you can see too well for me." "Ah! to be sure, sir. I take you——" "Could you see as well now if you had sixpence over one eye?" "Well, I don't know, sir, but I'm darned well sure I couldn't see at all if I'd another over t'other one."

* * * * *

Henry James, the American novelist, lives at Rye, one of the Cinque Ports, but recently he left Rye for a time and took a house in the country near the estate of a millionaire jam manufacturer, retired. This man, having married an earl's daughter, was ashamed of the trade whereby he had piled up his fortune.

The jam manufacturer one day wrote Mr. James an impudent letter, vowing that it was outrageous the way the James servants were trespassing on his grounds. Mr. James wrote back:

> "*Dear Sir*: I am very sorry to hear that my servants have been poaching on your preserves.
>
> "P.S.—You'll excuse my mentioning your preserves, won't you?"

* * * * *

An Omaha man was taking an automobile trip through the ranching section of the State, and to save time took a short cut over a bad stretch of road, full of jolts and bumps. During the afternoon his machine broke down, and, as the monkey wrench was missing from his tool kit, he started on foot for the nearest ranch house to borrow one. On arriving he found the farmer repairing his fence.

"Have you a monkey wrench about here that I can use?" he asked.

"Ay tank not," replied the farmer. "Yonson in nax saction ha kape cattle ranch, Svenson down har ha kape sheep ranch. Faller bane big fool to make monkey ranch in dese place."

* * * * *

Andrew Carnegie is fond of the Scots' national instrument, the bagpipe, and when he is at home at Skibo Castle usually has his pet piper to play for him at dinner. Particularly is the musician in attendance when the great philanthropist has guests.

On one occasion a big company of men sat down to table, and the piper pranced up and down the room as he played.

The whole thing was new to a French literary man, who politely asked the guest on his right, "Why does he walk up and down when he does this thing? Does it add to the volume of the sound, or does it make a cadence?"

"No," said the other, "I don't think it's that. I fancy it's to prevent the listeners getting his range with a knife or a water bottle."

* * * * *

Some time ago Professor Brander Matthews went to dine at a certain dramatic club in New York. Going to the club letter box he picked up and perused a letter which seemed to be addressed to him. It was a request from a tailor for the settlement of his little bill. As the man's name was quite strange to him he made a careful examination, and finding that he had been mistaken, put the missive back into its place. Immediately afterward he saw the real owner take possession of it, walk into the reading-room, read it carefully, and tear it into shreds. Then, assured of an audience, the man whose clothes were still unpaid for, assumed the weary smile of an accomplished ladykiller and remarked audibly, "Poor, silly, little girl!"

* * * * *

A street-car "masher" tried in every way to attract the attention of the pretty young girl opposite him. Just as he had about given up, the girl, entirely unconscious of what had been going on, happened to glance in his direction. The "masher" immediately took fresh courage.

"It's cold out to-day, isn't it?" he ventured.

The girl smiled and nodded assent, but had nothing to say.

"My name is Specknoodle," he volunteered.

"Oh, I am so sorry," she said sympathetically, as she left the car.

* * * * *

A Jew crossing the Brooklyn Bridge met a friend who said, "Abe, I'll bet you ten dollars that I can tell you exactly what you're thinking about."

"Vell," agreed Abe, producing a greasy bill, "I'll haf to take dot bet. Put up your money."

The friend produced two fives. "Abe," he said, "you are thinking of going over to Brooklyn, buying a small stock of goods, renting a small store, taking out all the fire-insurance that you can possibly get, and then burning out. Do I win my bet?"

"Vell," replied Abe, "you don't egsactly vin, but the idea is worth de money. Take id."

* * * * *

Andrew Carnegie tells a good story illustrating the canniness of the Scot.

An Irish friend had insisted that a Scotchman should stay at his house, instead of at a hotel, and kept him there for a month, playing the host in detail, even to treating him to sundry visits to the theater, paying the cab fares and the rest. When the visitor was returning home, the Irishman saw him to the station, and they went together to have a last cigar.

"Now, look here," said the Scot, "I'll hae nae mair o' this. Here ye've been keepin' me at your hoose for a month, an' payin' for a' the amusements and cabs and so on—I tell you I'll stan' nae mair o' it! We'll just hae a toss for this one!"

* * * * *

"Uncle Joe" Cannon has a way of speaking his mind that is sometimes embarrassing to others. On one occasion an inexperienced young fellow was called upon to make a speech at a banquet at which Speaker Cannon was also present.

"Gentlemen," began the young fellow, "my opinion is that the generality of mankind in general is disposed to take advantage of the generality of — —"

"Sit down, son," interrupted "Uncle Joe." "You are coming out of the same hole you went in at."

* * * * *

It is a well-established fact that the average school-teacher experiences a great deal of difficulty when she attempts to enforce the clear pronunciation of the terminal "g" of each present participle.

"Robert," said the teacher of one of the lower classes during the progress of a reading exercise, "please read the first sentence."

A diminutive lad rose to his feet and, amid a series of labored gasps, breathed forth the following:

"See the horse runnin'."

"Don't forget the 'g,' Robert," admonished the teacher.

"Gee! See the horse runnin'."

* * * * *

Miss Jeannette Gilder was one of the ardent enthusiasts at the début of Tetrazzini. After the first act she rushed to the back of the house to greet one of her friends. "Don't you think she is a wonder?" she asked excitedly.

"She is a great singer unquestionably," responded her more phlegmatic friend, "but the registers of her voice are not so even as, for instance, Melba's."

"Oh, bother Melba," said Miss Gilder. "Tetrazzini gives infinitely more heat from her registers."

* * * * *

Walter Damrosch tells of a matron in Chicago who, in company with her young nephew, was attending a musical entertainment.

The selections were apparently entirely unfamiliar to the youth; but when the "Wedding March" of Mendelssohn was begun he began to evince more interest.

"That sounds familiar," he said. "I'm not strong on these classical pieces, but that's a good one. What is it?"

"That," gravely explained the matron, "is the 'Maiden's Prayer.'"

* * * * *

A messenger came tearing up to the White House in '63, and hurriedly gaining admission to Mr. Lincoln, informed him in great excitement that a large wagon train had been surprised a short way across the Potomac and a brigadier-general taken prisoner.

"Did they capture the train?" inquired Old Abe.

"No, sir, the regiment came up and saved it," answered the messenger, "but the general, Mr. President, is a prisoner."

"Oh, never mind that," said Lincoln. "I can make a dozen generals in a day, but mules cost $300 apiece."

* * * * *

Two men were riding together one day through Paris. One was exceedingly bright and clever, while the other was correspondingly dull. As is usually the case, the latter monopolized the conversation. The talk of the dullard had become almost unendurable, when his companion saw a man on the street far ahead yawning.

"Look," he exclaimed, "we are overheard!"

* * * * *

One afternoon Mrs. Murphy appeared at the settlement house, all dressed up in her best bonnet and shawl. A huge black and blue spot disfigured one side of her face, however, and one eye was nearly closed. "Why, Mrs. Murphy, what is the matter?" cried one of the teachers; and then, realizing that she might have asked a tactless question, she hastily turned it off, by saying, "Well, cheer up, you might be worse off." "Sure an' I might," responded the indignant Mrs. Murphy. "I might not be married at all!"

* * * * *

A young woman in Central Park overheard an old negress call to a piccaninny: "Come heah, Exy, Exy!"

"Excuse me, but that's a queer name for a baby, aunty?"

"Dat ain't her full name," explained the old woman with pride; "dat's jes' de pet name I calls for short. Dat chile got a mighty grand name. Her ma picked it out in a medicine book—yessum, de child's full name is Eczema."

* * * * *

Sir Richard Bethell, afterward Lord Westbury, with a suave voice and a stately manner, nevertheless had a way of bearing down the foe with almost savage wit. Once, in court, he had to follow a barrister who had delivered his remarks in very loud tones. "Now that the noise in court has subsided," murmured Bethell, "I will tell your Honor in two sentences the gist of the case."

* * * * *

The resemblance of the Rev. Robert Collyer to Henry Ward Beecher was often remarked. One day, when walking through Central Park, hat in hand, as the day was hot, at a sharp turn in the path he came upon an old lady seated on one of the park benches. At sight of him she jumped to her feet, exclaiming:

"Goodness me! This is not Mr. Beecher?"

"No, madam," Dr. Collyer answered, "it is not. I hope Mr. Beecher is in a cooler place."

* * * * *

It is not necessary that a lawyer should be eloquent to win verdicts, but he must have the tact which turns an apparent defeat to his own advantage. One of the most successful of verdict winners was Sir James Scarlett. His skill in turning a failure into a success was wonderful. In a breach-of-promise case the defendant, Scarlett's client, was alleged to have been cajoled into an engagement by the plaintiff's mother. She was a witness in behalf of her daughter, and completely baffled Scarlett, who cross-examined her. But in his argument he exhibited his tact by this happy stroke of advocacy: "You saw, gentlemen of the jury, that I was but a child in her hands. What must my client have been?"

* * * * *

He was a young man—a candidate for an agricultural constituency—and he was sketching in glowing colors to an audience of rural voters the happy life the laborer would lead under an administration for the propagation of sweetness and light. "We have not yet three acres and a cow, but it will come. Old-age pensions are still of the future, but they will come." Similarly every item of his comprehensive program was endorsed by the same parrot cry. Then he went on to talk of prison reforms. "I have not yet personally," he said, "been inside a criminal lunatic asylum." Then there was a voice from the back of the hall, "But it will come."

*****

The judge had had his patience sorely tried by lawyers who wished to talk and by men who wished to evade jury service.

"Shudge!" cried a little German in the jury box.

"What is it?" demanded the judge.

"I t'ink I like to go home to my wife," said the German.

"You can't," retorted the judge. "Sit down."

"But, shudge," persisted the German, "I don't t'ink I make a good shuror."

"You're the best in the box," said the judge. "Sit down."

"What box?" said the German.

"Jury box," said the judge.

"But, shudge," persisted the little German, "I don't speak good English."

"You don't have to speak any at all," said the judge. "Sit down."

The little German pointed at the lawyers to make his last desperate plea.

"Shudge," he said, "I don't make noddings of what these fellers say."

It was the judge's chance to get even for many annoyances.

"Neither can any one else," he said. "Sit down."

*****

A parson, diminutive in size and his head covered with hair of the most fiery hue, officiated one Sunday for a friend in a colliery village near Nottingham. The old-fashioned pulpit had a high desk over which the parson's red head was hardly visible. This was too much for a burly collier seated immediately under the pulpit, who when he heard the text, "I am the Light of the World," exclaimed to the clerk, "Push him up a bit higher, mate; don't let him burn in the socket."

*****

"Biddy," said Pat timidly, "did ye iver think o' marryin'?"'

"Shure, now," said Biddy, looking demurely at her shoe—"shure, now, the subject has niver entered me mind at all, at all."

"It's sorry Oi am," said Pat, and he turned away.

"Wan minute, Pat," said Biddy softly. "Ye've set me thinkin'."

*****

From a French journal comes this little anecdote of a tutor and his royal pupil.

The lesson was in Roman history, and the prince was unprepared.

"We come now to the Emperor Caligula. What do you know about him, prince?"

The question was followed by a silence that was becoming awkward when it was broken by the diplomatic tutor. "Your highness is right," he said, "perfectly right. The less said about this emperor the better."

* * * * *

The following copies of queer advertisements have been collected and printed by club women:

"Bulldog for sale; will eat anything; is very fond of children."

"Lost—Near Highgate Archway, an umbrella belonging to a gentleman with a bent rib and a bone handle."

"Mr. Brown, furrier, begs to announce that he will make up gowns, capes and so forth, for ladies out of their own skin."

"Wanted, a herder for 500 sheep that can speak Spanish fluently."

"For Sale—House in good neighborhood, by an invalid lady three stories high and heated with furnace."

A contemporary contains the startling news that "A carload of brick came in for a walk through the park."

* * * * *

An error for which nervousness may have been responsible was that made by the boy who was told to take the Bishop's shaving water to him one morning and cautioned to answer the Bishop's inquiry "Who's there?" by saying, "The boy, my Lord." Whether from nervousness or not, the boy managed to transpose the words of this sentence with ludicrous effect, and the Bishop was surprised and perhaps alarmed to hear in response to his inquiry the answer, "The Lord, my boy."

* * * * *

Tailor—"Do you want padded shoulders, my little man?"

Willie—"Naw; pad de pants! Dat's where I need it most."

* * * * *

Dr. Tupper does not hesitate to take examples from his own profession, as witness his curious story of the young clergyman who, after preaching a funeral sermon, wished to invite the mourners to view the remains, but became confused and exclaimed:

"We will now pass around the bier."

* * * * *

"Wossatchoogot?"

"Afnoonnoos. Lassdition."

"Enthinkinnut?"

"Naw. Nothninnut 'cept lasspeechrosefelt's. Lottarot."

"Donsayso? Wosswetherpredickshun?"

"Sesrain. Donbleevetho. Funthingthiswethernevkintellwossgunnado."

"Thasright!"

* * * * *

President Eliot of Harvard recently visited a hotel in New York, and when he left the dining-room the colored man in charge of the hats picked up his tile without hesitation and handed it to him.

"How did you know that was my hat when you have a hundred there?" asked Mr. Eliot.

"I didn't know it, sah," said the negro.

"Didn't know it was mine? Then why did you give it to me?"

"Because you gave it to me, sah."

* * * * *

"How small have you felt?" she asked anxiously.

"Well," he replied, "I have felt as small as a man in the presence of the head plumber."

"That isn't enough."

"I have felt as small as the Prohibition nominee for Vice-President."

She shook her head.

"Or as a man when his wife catches him in a lie."

"That isn't anything."

"I have felt as small as the man who made a righteous complaint to the president of a trolley line."

She shook her head again sadly.

"That isn't anything to the way I feel," she said. "You know I have never been to Europe, and I've been talking with a girl who has just returned."

* * * * *

In one of the Atlanta Sunday-schools recently the lesson for the day had to do with Mammon and the corrupting influences of great riches.

Toward the close of the exercises the superintendent called upon the infant class to repeat the Golden Text, which had special reference to man's inability to serve his Creator and the money-god at one and the same time. The class failed to respond as it should, when the superintendent, noticing his own young hopeful in the ranks, who had that very morning been drilled thoroughly on the text, called on him. The response was immediate, though a slight departure from the original, for in a voice that was distinctly heard in all parts of the room there came the following modification:

"Ye can not serve God and mama!"

* * * * *

"Any complaints, corporal?" said the colonel, making one morning a personal inspection.

"Yes, sir. Taste that, sir," said the corporal promptly.

The colonel put the liquid to his lips. "Why," he said, "that's the best soup I ever tasted!"

"Yes, sir," said the corporal, "and the cook wants to call it coffee."

* * * * *

Reporter—"To what do you attribute your great age?"

Oldest Inhabitant—"I hain't sure yet, sir. There be several o' them patent-medicine companies as is bargainin' with me."

* * * * *

Mr. Choate, ex-Ambassador of the United States at London, tells of the address made by an Irish officer to his men who had just returned from a fruitless expedition.

Rising to his feet with the utmost solemnity and seriousness, the officer said:

"My men, I am fully aware of the fact that many of you brave fellows are disappointed because in this campaign you were afforded little opportunity to fight; but, my brave boys, reflect upon this: that had there been any fighting, there would have been many absent faces here to-day!"

* * * * *

"Young man (23) with five years' experience in leading publishers, desires to better his position."

But what better position could there be than that of leading our publishers?

* * * * *

From Children's Chat, by "Grandma" in the "Times" of Natal:

"I want you, my dears, to write me a short snake story, something that really happened to some one you know; and if you can tell me of a child being really bitten I shall be glad to hear about it."

Truly it is said that a child's best friend is his grandma.

* * * * *

Wandering over Salisbury Plain on Whit Monday, a correspondent came across a large stone inscribed: "Turn me over." After much difficulty he succeeded in turning it over, and found on the under side of the stone the words: "Now turn me back again, so that I can catch some other idiot."

* * * * *

He—"Dearest, if I had known this tunnel was so long, I'd have given you a jolly hug."

She—"Didn't you? Why—why—"

* * * * *

Timid Lady (going up the Washington Monument elevator).—"Conductor, what if the rope breaks that holds us?"

Conductor—"Oh, there are a number more attached as safety ropes."

Timid Lady—"But if they all break, where shall we go?"

Conductor—"Oh, well, m'm, that all depends upon what kind of a life you have been living before."

* * * * *

Elmer, though only a little boy, was the oldest child of an already numerous family. He was invited to go in and see a little baby sister. Asked by his mother what he thought of the baby, he said, "W'y, mama, it's real nice. But do you think we needed it?"

* * * * *

Time: 2 A.M.

"Ma, I want a drink!"

"Hush, darling; turn over and go to sleep."

"I want a drink!"

"No, you are restless. Turn over, dear, and go to sleep."

(After five minutes.) "Ma, I want a drink."

"Lie still, Ethel, and go to sleep."

"But I want a drink!"

"No, you don't want a drink; you had a drink just before you went to bed. Now be still and go right to sleep."

(After five minutes.) "Ma, won't you please give me a drink?"

"If you say another word I'll get up and spank you. Now go to sleep. You are a naughty girl."

(After two minutes.) "Ma, when you get up to spank me will you give me a drink?"

* * * * *

Once upon a time there was a young married man who had some slight bickerings with the woman of his choice. These having occurred with great frequency, he went to his father, who was older and much more married.

"Father," he said, "is it not meet that I should be the ringmaster in my own wickiup? Or must I kowtow to the old lady?"

Whereat the old man smiled wisely and said:

"My son, yonder are a hundred chickens and here a fine team of horses. Do you place the feathered tribe on this wagon, hitch up the team, and start out. Wherever you find a man and his wife living together, make diligent investigation to find out who the commanding officer is, and where it is the woman give her a chicken. If you find a man running a house give him one of the horses."

So the young man loaded up the fowls and started out upon his pilgrimage of self-education. And when he had but seven chickens left, he approached a habitation with his forlorn inquiry, to which the man replied:

"I'm the ace-high cockalorum of this outfit."

And the wife, without fear or favor, corroborated the statement. Then the young man said:

"Take your choice of the horses. Either one you fancy is yours." And after the man had walked around the team several times and looked in their mouths, he said, "Well, I'll take the bay."

Now, the wife didn't like bay horses, and she called John aside, and after whispering in his ear she allowed him to return.

"I guess I'll take the black horse," he said.

"Not a bit of it," said the pilgrim. "You'll take a chicken."

* * * * *

They were talking over the engagement of one of the daughters of the family when the negro servant came in. One of the girls asked: "Cindy, have you seen Edith's fiancé?" "No'm, honey, hit ain't been in de wash yit."

* * * * *

In the late financial stringency a clerk in one of the New York banks was trying to explain to a stolid old Dutchman why the bank could not pay cash to depositors as formerly, and was insisting that he be satisfied with Clearing House checks. But the old man could not grasp the situation, and finally the president of the bank was called upon to enlighten the dissatisfied customer. After a detailed explanation of the financial situation the president concluded, "Now, my good man, you understand, don't you?"

"Yes," dubiously replied the Dutchman, "I tinks I understand. It's just like this; ven my baby vakes up in der night und cries for milk, I give her a milk ticket."

* * * * *

Levinsky, despairing of his life, made an appointment with a famous specialist. He was surprised to find fifteen or twenty people in the waiting-room.

After a few minutes he leaned over to a gentleman near him and whispered, "Say, mine frient, this must be a pretty goot doctor, ain't he?"

"One of the best," the gentleman told him.

Levinsky seemed to be worrying over something.

"Vell, say," he whispered again, "he must be pretty exbensive, then, ain't he? Vat does he charge?"

The stranger was annoyed by Levinsky's questions and answered rather shortly: "Fifty dollars for the first consultation and twenty-five dollars for each visit thereafter."

"Mine Gott!" gasped Levinsky. "Fifty tollars the first time und twenty-five tollars each time afterwards!"

For several minutes he seemed undecided whether to go or to wait. "Und twenty-five tollars each time afterward," he kept muttering. Finally, just as he was called into the office, he was seized with a brilliant inspiration. He rushed toward the doctor with outstretched hands.

"Hello, doctor," he said effusively. "Vell, here I am again."

* * * * *

A clergyman who was holding a children's service at a Continental winter resort had occasion to catechize his hearers on the parable of the unjust steward. "What is a steward?" he asked. A little boy who had arrived from England a few days before held up his hand. "He is a man, sir," he replied, "who brings you a basin."

* * * * *

A teacher giving a lecture on the rhinoceros found his class was not giving him all the attention it should. "Now, gentlemen," he said, "if you want to realize the true hideous nature of this animal you must keep your eyes fixed on me."

* * * * *

A negro had made several ineffectual efforts to propose to the object of his affections, but on each occasion his courage failed him at the last moment. After thinking the matter over he finally decided to telephone, which he did. "Is that you, Samantha?" he inquired upon being given the proper number. "Yes, it's me," returned the lady. "Will you marry me, Samantha, and marry me quick?" "Yes, I will," was the reply; "who's speaking?"

* * * * *

He was a big, black, good-hearted, old negro, stranded near Boston, and he had decided, after considerable "cogitation," to work his way back to, the South, where he would feel more at home. In Boston, in Springfield, in Hartford, in New Haven, it was always the same. When he rang a bell and asked for work and a bite to eat the answer usually was, "I'm very sorry, but there's not a thing to be done here to-day." There were occasional exceptions, of course, or uncle could never have got on, but the thing most to be counted upon was pleasing politeness coupled with nothing else.

At last the old man left New York and then Philadelphia behind, and one day found himself in Baltimore. His knowledge of geography was *nil*, but he thought he ought soon to be getting into "de Souf," and with that hope at heart rang the bell of a fine house on Charles Street. The door was opened by the host himself, who, after an instant's survey of the figure before him, blurted out:

"Why, yo' — — black rascal! How dare yo' ring this bell? Get off mah steps this secon', befo' I brek yo' haid!"

"'Deed I will, boss; 'deed I will," came the hurried answer. "I wuz on'y lookin' fer a bite to eat, boss."

"A bite to eat!" repeated the other. "An' don't yo' know whar to go for all yo' want? Get yo'self round back, an' they'll feed yo' full—but cyart yo' good-for-nuthin' black carcass off these steps, I say."

And as uncle went around to the side door he raised his hands to heaven, and with tears of rejoicing running down his furrowed cheeks, said:

"Bress de Lord! I's back agin among mah own folks!"

* * * * *

A little boy who had just joined Sunday-school was asked by his mother how he liked it.

"Why!" exclaimed Charlie disgustedly, "they don't know much. The teacher asked what was the collec', and I was the only one who knew."

"And what did you say, dear?"

"Why, I told them pretty quick that it was a pain in the stomach."

* * * * *

Travelers' tales which often add charm to the conversation of an agreeable person frequently render a bore more tiresome than ever, a fact that was amusingly illustrated by an occurrence in a Baltimore clubhouse not long ago.

"There I stood, gentlemen," the long-winded narrator was saying, after droning on for an hour with reference to his trip to Switzerland—"there I stood, with the abyss yawning in front of me."

"Pardon me," hastily interjected one of the unfortunate men who had been obliged to listen to the story, "but was that abyss yawning before you got there?"

* * * * *

After a lesson on digestion the teacher, anxious to know how much her instruction had been understood, questioned the class. The first answer was rather discouraging, as the girl called upon made this startling statement:

"Digestion begins in the mouth and ends in the big and little testament."

It was the same teacher who received the following note:

"Pleas teacher do not tel Mary any more about her incides it makes her so proud."

* * * * *

When Sam Jones was holding his meetings in Dallas, on one occasion he said: "There's no such thing as a perfect man. Anybody present who has ever known a perfect man stand up."

Nobody stood up.

"Those who have ever known a perfect woman, stand up."

One demure little woman stood up.

"Did you ever know an absolutely perfect woman?" asked Sam, somewhat amazed.

"I didn't know her personally," replied the little old woman, "but I have heard a great deal about her. She was my husband's first wife."

* * * * *

Former President Scott, of the Cincinnati Southern Railroad, was greatly annoyed, when he first took hold of the road, by the claims for horses and cattle killed by trains on their way through Kentucky. It seemed as though it were not possible for a train to run north or south through Kentucky without killing either a horse or a cow. And every animal killed, however scrawny, scrubby, or miserable it may have been before the accident, always figured in the claims subsequently presented as of the best blood in Kentucky. "Well," said Scott one day, after examining a claim, "I don't know anything that improves stock in Kentucky like crossing it with a locomotive."

* * * * *

One of a loving couple (watching a pile-driver at work)—"Dear, I feel so sorry for those poor men. They have been trying for the last half hour to lift that thing out, and every time they get it almost to the top, it falls back again."

* * * * *

Sentinel (on guard)—"Halt! Who comes there?"

The Colonel—"Fool!"

Sentinel—"Advance, fool, and give the countersign."

* * * * *

"Oh, I'm so sorry I could not come to your 'At Home' yesterday."

"Dear me, weren't you there?"

"Why of course I was—how very silly of me—I quite forgot."

* * * * *

A theological student was sent one Sunday to supply a vacant pulpit in a Connecticut valley town. A few days after he received a copy of the weekly paper of that place with the following item marked:

"Rev. — — of the senior class at Yale Seminary supplied the pulpit at the Congregational Church last Sunday, and the church will now be closed three weeks for repairs."

* * * * *

A Certain Ohio lady with a large sense of religious duty was recently importuned by a tramp. The good religionist, after considerable hesitation, produced a piece of dry bread which she delivered with the following formula, evidently prepared for such occasion:

"Now, sir, not for your sake, nor for my sake, but for God's sake, I give you this bread."

The tramp accepted the offering and had got as far as the gate when he suddenly turned and came back where his benefactress was waiting to see him safely out.

"Say, miss," he drawled, "not for your sake, nor for my sake, but for God's sake put some butter on it."

* * * * *

"Mother, mother, mother, turn the hose on me!" sang little Willie, as his mama was dressing him one morning.

"What do you mean?" she asked.

"You've put my stockin's on wrong side out," he said.

* * * * *

The will of Stephen Girard provided that no clergyman should ever be allowed to enter the splendid Girard College at Philadelphia.

One day a very clerical looking man, with immaculate white cravat and choker, approached the entrance.

"You can't come in here," said the janitor.

"The — — I can't!" said the stranger.

"Oh," said the janitor, "excuse me. Step right in."

It is said that the visitor was the late State Senator Sessions, of Western New York.

* * * * *

The following anecdote of ex-President Roosevelt's youth is told:

When Roosevelt was a student at Harvard he was required to recite a poem in public declamation. He got as far as a line which read:

"When Greece her knees in suppliance bent," when he stuck there.

Again he tried:

"When Greece her knees...," but could get no farther.

The teacher waited patiently, finally remarking:

"Grease her knees again, Roosevelt, then perhaps she'll go."

* * * * *

A Young graduate in law, who had had some experience in New York City, wrote to a prominent practitioner in Arkansas to inquire what chance there was in that section for such a one as he described himself to be. He said: "I am a Republican in politics, and an honest young lawyer." The reply that came seemed encouraging in its interest: "If you are a Republican the game laws here will protect you, and if you are an honest lawyer you will have no competition."

* * * * *

Brown—"Ah! they've just dropped the anchor."

Mrs. B.—"And served 'em right! It's been dangling outside all the morning!"

* * * * *

As the immaculate young woman and the tired but happy-looking young man entered the Pullman, followed by a grinning porter, the other passengers became "wise" in a moment. The stout drummer leaned over to the man behind him and remarked:

"Bride and groom—100 to 1."

Every one turned to view the newcomers, who had deposited themselves vis-à-vis in No. 4. As if unconscious of any scrutiny, the young man said, in a high, nasal voice:

"Well, do as you like about it; either increase the margin or let it go. You didn't follow my advice in the first place, but if you want to pull out, you'd better do it now."

"Oh, I know," the woman replied. "What's the use of going all over it again?"

"Huh!" said the stout man's companion. "Guess you lose. Been playing the market. Not much bride and groom talk in that."

The rest of the passengers sniffed and then turned their backs on the new couple. Whereat the young man smiled at the young woman, and they softly joined hands as he whispered:

"Millicent, dear, my shoes are full of rice."

* * * * *

A Short time ago an old lady went on board Nelson's flag-ship, the *Victory*. The different objects of interest were duly shown her, and on reaching the spot where the great naval hero was wounded (which is marked by a raised brass plate), the officer remarked: "Here Nelson fell." "And no wonder!" exclaimed the old lady; "I nearly fell there myself."

* * * * *

A Good Samaritan, passing an apartment-house in the small hours of the morning, noticed a man leaning limply against the doorway.

"What's the matter?" he asked. "Drunk?"

"Yep."

"Do you live in this house?"

"Yep."

"Do you want me to help you upstairs?"

"Yep."

With much difficulty he half dragged, half carried the drooping figure up the stairway to the second floor.

"What floor do you live on?" he asked. "Is this it?"

"Yep."

Rather than face an irate wife who might, perhaps, take him for a companion more at fault than her spouse, he opened the first door he came to and pushed the limp figure in.

The good Samaritan groped his way downstairs again. As he was passing through the vestibule he was able to make out the dim outlines of another man, apparently in worse condition than the first one.

"What's the matter?" he asked. "Are you drunk, too?"

"Yep," was the feeble reply.

"Do you live in this house, too?"

"Yep."

"Shall I help you upstairs?"

"Yep."

Stopping on the second floor, where this man also said he lived, he opened the door and pushed him in. As he again reached the front door he discerned the shadow of a third man, evidently worse off than either of the other two. He was about to approach him when the object of his solicitude lurched out into the street and threw himself into the arms of a passing policeman. "For Heaven's sake, off'cer," he gasped, "protect me from that man. He's done nothin' all night long but carry me upstairs 'n' throw me down th' elevator shaf'."

* * * * *

Husband comes in to find his wife turning everything topsy-turvy.

"Good gracious! Isabel, what are you doing?"

"I just received a telegram from Aunt Jane saying she'll be here at 6.30 and I can't find her photograph anywhere."

* * * * *

At the school at which the writer was educated there was a certain assistant master who invariably "put his foot in it" when he got the chance. On one occasion, being exasperated by the conduct of a boy, he turned to him and said, "Look here, X., I'll take care that you won't be the biggest fool in the class as long as I'm here."

* * * * *

Mrs. Barron was one of the new "summer folk," and not acquainted with the vernacular. Consequently, she was somewhat surprised, upon sending an order for a roast of lamb to the nearest butcher, to receive the following note in reply: "Dear Mam. I am sorry I have not killed myself this week, but I can get you a leg off my brother (the butcher at the farther end of the town). He's full up of what you want. I seen him last night with five legs. Yours respectful. George Gunton."

*****

An artist employed in repairing the properties of an old church in Belgium, being refused payment in a lump sum, was asked for details, and sent in his bill as follows:-

1.	Corrected the Ten Commandments,	£1	10	0
2.	Embellished Pontius Pilate and put a ribbon in his bonnet,	0	8	1
3.	Put a New Tail on the Rooster of St. Peter and mended his Comb,	0	12	0
4.	Re-plumed and Gilded the Left Wing of the Guardian Angel,	0	15	6
5.	Washed the Servant of the High Priest and put carmine on his cheek,	0	1	0
6.	Renewed Heaven, adjusted two Stars, and cleaned the Moon,	1	16	0
7.	Re-animated the Flames of Purgatory and restored Souls,	6	7	0
8.	Revived the Flames of Hell, put a New Tail on the Devil, mended his left hoof, and did several jobs for the damned,	1	16	6
9.	Re-bordering the Robe of Herod and re-adjusting his Wig,	0	17	3
10.	Put new Spotted Dashes on the Son of Tobias and dressing on his sack	0	7	6
11.	Cleaned the Ears of Balaam's Ass and shod him,	0	9	0
12.	Put Earrings in the Ears of Sarah,	0	9	2
13.	Put a New Stone in David's Sling, enlarged the Head of Goliath, and extended his Legs,	0	8	8
14.	Decorated Noah's Ark,	0	17	6
15.	Mended the Shirt of the Prodigal Son and cleaned his ears,	0	15	3
	—*P. Sylvester, Summerfield, Warham Road, Croydon.*	£17	10	5

*****

Shortly after two o'clock one bitter winter morning a physician drove four miles in answer to a telephone call. On his arrival the man who had summoned him said:

"Doctor, I ain't in any particular pain, but somehow or other I've got a feeling that death is nigh."

The doctor felt the man's pulse and listened to his heart.

"Have you made your will?"

The man turned pale.

"Why, no, doctor, at my age—oh, Doc, it ain't true is it? It can't be true!"

"Who's your lawyer?"

"Higginbotham."

"Well, you'd better send for him at once."

The patient, white and trembling, went to the 'phone.

"Who's your pastor?" continued the doctor.

"The Rev. Kellogg M. Brown," mumbled the patient. "But, doctor, do you think—"

"Send for him immediately. Your father, too, should be summoned; also your—"

"Say, doctor, do you really think I'm going to die?" The man began to blubber softly.

The doctor looked at him hard.

"No, I don't," he replied grimly. "There's nothing at all the matter with you. But I'd hate to be the only man you've made a fool of on a night like this."

* * * * *

Dr. L. E. Wilson, a wealthy young Baltimore physician, was awakened one stormy night by a man who declared the doctor's services were wanted three miles out in the country. Just before the doctor called up the stable for his horse, the visitor asked what the charge would be. "Three dollars," was the reply. When the house containing the supposed patient was reached, the man alighted first, and, handing the doctor three dollars, remarked: "That will be all, doctor. I couldn't find a hackman who would do it for less than six dollars."

* * * * *

A certain prosy preacher recently gave an endless discourse on the prophets. First he dwelt at length on the minor prophets. At last he finished them, and the congregation gave a sigh of relief. He took a long breath and continued: "Now I shall proceed to the major prophets."

After the major prophets had received more than ample attention the congregation gave another sigh of relief.

"Now that I have finished with the minor prophets and the major prophets, what about Jeremiah? Where is Jeremiah's place?"

At this point a tall man arose in the back of the church. "Jeremiah can have my place," he said; "I'm going home."

* * * * *

Any one who has traveled on the New York subway in rush hours can easily appreciate the following:

A little man, wedged into the middle of a car, suddenly thought of pickpockets, and quite as suddenly remembered that he had some money in his overcoat. He plunged his hand into his pocket and was somewhat shocked upon encountering the fist of a fat fellow-passenger.

"Aha" snorted the latter. "I caught you that time!"

"Leggo!" snarled the little man. "Leggo my hand!"

"Pickpocket!" hissed the fat man.

"Scoundrel!" retorted the little one.

Just then a tall man in their vicinity glanced up from his paper.

"I'd like to get off here," he drawled, "if you fellows don't mind taking your hands out of my pocket."

* * * * *

Aunt Mahaly, an old negress with a worthless husband, was relating her troubles to her minister. The usual condolences were offered by the latter and remedies suggested, but at each one Aunt Mahaly shook a doubting head—she had tried them all without avail.

The minister sighed and pondered, and at last had an inspiration. He leaned to Aunt Mahaly, who brightened visibly.

"Sis' Mahaly," he said, "hab you eber tried heapin' coals er fire on his haid?"

The gleam of hope faded from Aunt Mahaly's face.

"No, Bre'r Jackson, I ain't never done dat, but I's tried po'in' hot water ovuh him."

* * * * *

A barber in South Bend, having been out late the night before, had a shaky hand the next morning and cut a patron's cheek four times. After each accident the barber said, as he sponged away the blood: "Oh, dear me, how careless!"

The patron took all these gashes in grave silence. But when the shave was over he filled a glass at the water-cooler, took a mouthful of water, and, with compressed lips, proceeded to shake his head from side to side.

"What is the matter?" the barber asked. "You ain't got the toothache, have you?"

"No," said the customer; "I only wanted to see if my mouth would still hold water without leaking."

* * * * *

At one of the lectures by Professor George Kirchwey, dean of Columbia Law College, New York, the students were uneasy. There was something wrong in the air. Books were dropped, chairs were pushed along the floor. There were various interruptions. The nerves of all were on edge. The members of the class kept their eyes on the clock and awaited the conclusion of the hour of the lecture. The clock beat Professor Kirchwey by perhaps a minute, but at the expiration of the schedule time the students started to their feet and prepared to leave. "Wait a minute," objected Professor Kirchwey; "don't go just yet. I have a few more pearls to cast."

* * * * *

Mrs. Flint *always* demanded instant and unquestioning obedience from her children. One afternoon a storm came up and she sent her son John to close the trapdoor leading to the roof.

"But mother—" said John.

"John, I told you to shut the trapdoor."

"Yes, but, Mother—"

"John, shut that trapdoor."

"All right, Mother, if you say so, but—"

"John!"

John slowly climbed the stairs and shut the trapdoor. The storm howled and raged. Two hours later the family gathered for tea. When the meal was half over Aunt Mary had not appeared, and Mrs. Flint started an investigation. She did not have to ask many questions; John answered the first one:

"Please, Mother, she is up on the roof."

* * * * *

An absent-minded scientist, in the employ of the government at Washington, recently met his physician in the street.

"I don't know what's the matter with me, Doctor," said the man of science. "I am limping badly to-day. Do you think it's locomotor ataxia?"

"Scarcely that," replied the physician. "You are walking with one foot on the curb and the other in the gutter."

* * * * *

One Sunday John Wanamaker visited the Sunday-school classes in which he was greatly interested, and after talking the lesson over told the pupils he would try to answer any questions the boys or girls wanted to ask him.

One little girl raised her hand, and spoke out timidly: "Will you please tell me, Mr. Wanamaker, how much those large French dolls are that you have in your show-window?"

* * * * *

Judge—"Have you been arrested before?"

Prisoner—"No, sir."

Judge—"Have you been in this court before?"

Prisoner—"No, sir."

Judge—"Are you certain?"

Prisoner—"I am, sir."

Judge—"But your face looks decidedly familiar. Where have I seen it before?"

Prisoner—"I'm the bartender in the saloon across the way, sir."

* * * * *

Henry Guy Carleton, wit, journalist, and playwright, has an impediment in his speech about which he is not in the least sensitive. Meeting Nat Goodwin one day he asked:

"G-g-goodwin, c-c-an you g-g-give m-m-me f-f-fifteen m-m-minutes?"

"Certainly," replied the comedian, "what is it?"

"I w-w-want to have f-f-five m-m-minutes' c-c-conversation with you."

* * * * *

A German pedler rapped timidly at the kitchen entrance. Mrs. Kelly, angry at being interrupted in her washing, flung open the door and glowered at him.

"Did yez wish to see me?" she demanded in threatening tones.

The pedler backed off a few steps.

"Vell, if I did," he assured her with an apologetic grin, "I got my vish, thank you."

* * * * *

A lady from South America possessed of a decidedly quick temper came to New York with a very incomplete knowledge of the English language. At her hotel she rang for the chambermaid. But a waiter came instead. Having ascertained that the name of the chambermaid was Susan, the lady marshaled her meager knowledge of English in a desperate effort to make the waiter understand that he should call the chambermaid. What she said to him, however, was:

"Call me Susan!"

The waiter leaned against the wall much alarmed.

"Call me Susan!" shouted the South American.

The waiter became appalled.

"Call me Susan!" roared the lady, her eyes flashing furiously.

"Susan, then—if you will have it!" exclaimed the poor waiter. Then he fled precipitately.

* * * * *

"Please, mum," began the aged hero in appealing tones, as he stood at the kitchen-door on washday, "I've lost my leg—"

"Well, I ain't got it," snapped the woman, slamming the door.

* * * * *

In the absence of the regularly appointed spokesman, Mr. Makinbrakes had reluctantly consented to make a presentation speech.

"Miss Higham," he said, "unfortunately it is my—er—fortunate lot to fulfill the embarrassing—the pleasant duty of—of inflicting a few remarks upon this occasion—which is highly appreciated, I assure you, and by none more so than myself, for the reason that—in short, as I may say, it falls to my lot to convey, so to speak, the assurances of—that is, with the assurances of those to whom—to whom I have occasion to refer to—more or less—in this connection, together with the best wishes, if I may so express myself, of those who have clubbed together—who have associated themselves—not that you need anything of the kind, of course, but as a token of—as a token of—of—with which few remarks, Miss Higham, it is my—my pleasant surprise to hand you this gold watch and chain. I—I thank you."

* * * * *

The reputed affinity between the Southern negro and unguarded poultry is the subject of a story told by Senator Bacon, of Georgia. An old colored man, notorious for his evil ways, after attending a revival meeting, desired to lead a better life. At a later meeting he was called up to be questioned.

"Well, Rastus," said the revivalist, "I hope you are now trying to live a Christian life in accordance with the rules of the Church. Have you been stealing any chickens lately?"

"No, sah! I ain't stole no chicken ob late."

"Any turkeys or pigs?"

Rastus, grieved, replied: "No, sah!"

"I am very glad to hear that you have been doing better lately," replied the evangelist. "Continue to lead a holy and Christian life, Rastus."

After the meeting was over, Rastus drew a long breath of relief, and turning to his wife exclaimed:

"Mandy, if he'd said ducks I'd been a lost nigger, suah!"

* * * * *

The late Moses Coit Tyler, so long Professor of History in Cornell, was at one time a popular professor in the University of Michigan. One raw February morning as he was calling the roll of an 8 o'clock class in English, he called "Mr. Robbins," and receiving no answer called again: "Mr. Robbins?" Still no reply. "Ah," said Professor Tyler, looking around upon the class in his inimitable manner, "it is rather early for robins."

* * * * *

He—"Isn't dinner ready yet?"

She—"No, dear. I got it according to the time you set the clock when you came in last night, and dinner will be ready in four hours."

* * * * *

A foreigner, meeting an American friend, said to him, "How are you?" The latter replied, "Out of sight."

The man considered this very clever, and decided to use the expression on the next occasion. Shortly after he was met by a friend, who asked, "How are you?"

With visible pride he answered, "You don't see me."

* * * * *

There is a clerk in the employ of a Philadelphia business man who, while a fair worker, is yet an individual of pronounced eccentricity.

One day a wire basket fell off the top of the clerk's desk and scratched his cheek. Not having any court plaster at hand, he slapped on three two-cent postage stamps and continued his work.

A few minutes later he had occasion to take some papers to his employer's private office. When he entered, the "old man" observing the postage stamps on his cheek fixed him with an astonished stare. "Look here, Jenkins!" he exclaimed. "You are carrying too much postage for second-class matter!"

* * * * *

"I suppose," said the facetious stranger, watching a workman spread a carpet from the church door to the curb, "that's the high road to heaven you're fixing there?"

"No," replied the man; "this is merely a bridal path."

* * * * *

"I hope my little Tommy has taken to heart mama's talk of last night about charity and usefulness," said a fond mother. "How many acts of kindness has he done? How many hearts has my Tommy made grateful and glad?"

Her Tommy replied:

"I've done a lot of good, ma; I gave your new hat to a beggar woman, and I gave the cook's shoes to a little girl in busted rubbers what I seen on the street, and I gave a poor, lame shoe-string seller pa's black suit, the open front one that he hardly ever wears."

* * * * *

Charles Francis Adams was escorting a literary friend about Boston. They were viewing the different objects of attraction and finally came to Bunker Hill. They stood looking at the splendid monument when

Adams remarked: "This is the place, sir, where Warren fell."

"Ah!" replied the Englishman, evidently not very familiar with American history. "Was he seriously hurt by his fall?"

Mr. Adams looked at his friend. "Hurt!" said he. "He was killed, sir."

"Ah, indeed," the Englishman replied, still eying the monument and commencing to compute its height in his own mind. "Well, I should think he might have been—falling so far."

* * * * *

"Darling," said his bride, "I had a terrible feeling of sadness come over me this afternoon—a sort of feeling that you were doing something that would break my heart if I knew of it. Think, sweet, what were you doing this afternoon at four o'clock?"

"Dearest," replied her husband, tenderly and reassuringly, "at that hour I was licking stamps and pasting them on envelopes."

* * * * *

A few years ago a dear old lady, who formerly lived in Ipswich, and was a relative of the poet Whittier, had occasion to go on a journey which necessitated a night's ride in a sleeping car. Being subject to attacks of acute indigestion, she took the precaution to place a few leaves of the commercial mustard plaster in her hand bag.

During the night, pains, either real or imaginary, warned her of trouble and prevented sleep. Deciding upon the application of a plaster, she reached in the dark for the hand bag, and, having secured it, proceeded to put one of the leaves where it would do the most good, and immediately felt comforted and enjoyed a refreshing sleep until morning.

Upon removing the plaster, what was her astonishment to find that it was a $10 bank note that had brought such speedy relief.

* * * * *

Beerbohm Tree was once endeavoring to get a well-known actor back into his company. He invited the man to call and received him in his dressing room as he was making-up. "How much would you want to come back to me?" inquired Mr. Tree, busy with his paint pots. The other named an exorbitant salary to which Tree merely retorted as he went on making up: "Don't slam the door when you go out, will you?"

* * * * *

"Oh, mama," she cried, rushing into her mother's room, and flinging her arms around her mother's neck, "He loves me! He loves me!"

"My dear child, I'm so glad! Has he told you? Has he asked you to be his wife?"

"No, but he's down in the library learning to play chess with papa."

* * * * *

"If I had only known that this pleasure was in store for me," said the doctor, as he shook hands cordially with his wife's cousins, "I should certainly have arranged my business so as to be home earlier."

"Why, pa," piped up little Tommy, "don't you remember that ma told you they were coming, and you said, 'Oh, the devil!'"

* * * * *

A minister of a fashionable church had always left the greeting of strangers to be attended to by the ushers until he read some newspaper articles in reference to the matter.

"Suppose a representative should visit our church," said his wife. "Wouldn't it be awful?"

"It would," the minister admitted.

The following Sunday evening he noticed a plainly dressed woman in one of the free pews. She sat alone and was clearly not a member of the flock. After the benediction the minister hastened and intercepted her at the door.

"How do you do?" he said, offering his hand. "I am very glad to have you with us."

"Thank you," replied the young woman.

"I hope we may see you often in our church home," he went on. "We are always glad to welcome new faces."

"Yes, sir."

"Do you live in this parish?" he asked.

The girl looked blank.

"If you will give me your address my wife and I will call on you some evening."

"You wouldn't need to go far, sir," said the young woman. "I'm your cook."

* * * * *

The mission-workers on the East Side frequently see the humorous as well as the sadder side of life. A man prominent in reform work in New York City recounts the experience of a certain young woman, new to the task, who set about posting herself as to conditions in a neighborhood near Avenue A.

The ambitious missionary had entered the house of an Irishwoman, and had made some preliminary inquiries, when she was suddenly interrupted by the woman, who said:

"Say, youse is fresh at dis business, ain't youse?"

The amateur in mission work blushingly admitted such to be the case, adding, "I have never visited you before, Mrs. Muldoon."

"Thin," explained the Irishwoman, "I tell ye what to do. Ye sit down in that chair there, ye read me a short psalm, ye gives me fifty cints, an' thin ye goes."

* * * * *

The following conversation was overheard during a hunting trip in Scotland:

Fitz—"I say, are all your beaters out of the wood?"

Keeper—"Yes, sir."

Fitz—"Are you sure?"

Keeper—"Yes, sir."

Fitz—"Have you counted them?"

Keeper—"No, sir; but I know they're all right."

Fitz—"Then I've shot a deer!"

* * * * *

Joe—"I love you; I love you. Won't you be my wife?"

Jess—"You must see mama first."

Joe—"I have seen her several times, but I love you just the same."

* * * * *

Long after the victories of Washington over the French and English had made his name familiar to all Europe, Benjamin Franklin chanced to dine with the English and French Ambassadors, when the following toasts were drunk:

"'England'—The Sun, whose bright beams enlighten and fructify the remotest corners of the earth."

The French Ambassador, filled with national pride, but too polite to dispute the previous toast, offered the following:

"'France'—The Moon, whose mild, steady and cheering rays are the delight of all nations, consoling them in darkness and making their dreariness beautiful."

Doctor Franklin then arose, and, with his usual dignified simplicity, said:

"'George Washington'—The Joshua who commanded the Sun and Moon to stand still, and they obeyed him."

* * * * *

The following appeal of a Western editor is still going the rounds, although it is to be hoped that by this time the writer's only trouble is in having his vest made large enough:

"We see by an esteemed contemporary that a young lady in Chicago is so particular that she kneads bread with her gloves on. What of that? The editor of this paper needs bread with his coat on; he needs bread with his trousers on; in fact he needs bread with all of his clothes on. And if some of his debtors don't pay up pretty quick he'll need bread without anything at all on, and this Western climate is no Garden of Eden."

* * * * *

The unconscious humors of country journalism, says William Allen White, are often more amusing than the best efforts of the alleged "funny man."

According to Mr. White there once appeared in a Kansas paper the following "personal notice":

"Our prominent townsman Theodore Monkton is seriously ill. He is being attended twice a day by Doctor Smith, in consultation with Doctor Morgan. His recovery, therefore, is in great doubt."

* * * * *

A crowd of small boys were gathered about the entrance of a circus tent in one of the small cities in New Hampshire one day, trying to get a glimpse of the interior. A man standing near watched them for a few moments, then walking up to the ticket-taker he said:

"Let all these boys in, and count them as they pass."

The man did as requested, and when the last one had gone, he turned and said, "Twenty-eight."

"Good!" said the man, "I guessed just right," and walked off.

* * * * *

The editor of a rural newspaper determined to adopt the idea of posting bulletins on a bulletin board for all important events that happened in the town. Soon afterward he was told one morning by the local physician that Deacon Jones was seriously ill. The deacon was a man of some distinction in the community, so the editor posted a series of bulletins as follows:

10 A. M.—Deacon Jones no better.

11 A. M.—Deacon Jones has relapse.

12.30 P. M.—Deacon Jones weaker. Pulse failing.

1 P. M.—Deacon Jones has slight rally.

2.15 P. M.—Deacon Jones's family has been summoned.

3.10 P. M.—Deacon Jones has died and gone to heaven.

Later in the afternoon a traveling salesman happened by, stopped to read the bulletins, and going to the bulletin board, made another report concerning the deceased. It was:

4.10 P. M.—Great excitement in heaven. Deacon Jones has not yet arrived.

* * * * *

A group of drummers were trading yarns on the subject of hospitality, when one, a little Virginian with humorous eyes and a delightful drawl, took up his parable thus:

"I was down in Louisiana last month, travelin' 'cross country with a friend, when we kinder got lost in a mighty lonesome sort of road just about dark. We rode along a right good piece after sundown, and when we saw a light ahead, I tell you it looked first-rate. We drove up to the light, finding 'twas a house, and when I hollered like a lost calf the man came out and we asked him to take us in for the night. He looked at us mighty hard, then said:

"'Wal, I reckon I kin stand it if you kin.'

"So we went in and found 'twas only a two-room shanty, just swarmin' with children. He had six, from four to eleven years old; as there didn't seem to be but one bed, me an' Stony wondered what in thunder would become of us.

"They gave us supper, good hog and hominy, the best they had, and then the old woman put the two youngest kids to bed. They went straight to sleep. Then she took those out, laid them over in the corner, put the next two to bed, and so on.

"After all the children were asleep on the floor the old folk went in the other room and told us we could go to bed if we wanted to, and bein' powerful tired out, we did.

"Well, sir, the next morning when we woke up we were lying over in the corner with the kids, and the old man and the old woman had the bed."

* * * * *

"Waiter, what have you got?" said May Irwin in one of her plays.

"Well, I've got pig's feet—"

"Never mind telling me your troubles, I want to know what you've got to eat?"

* * * * *

As every one knows, the great Von Moltke never wasted words and despised anything that approached garrulity in others. German army officers are fond of telling an anecdote illustrative of this peculiarity:

Von Moltke was leaving Berlin on a railway journey. Just before the train pulled out of the station a captain of hussars entered the general's compartment and, recognizing him, saluted with "Guten Morgen, Excellenz!"

Two hours later the train slowed up at a way station. The captain arose, saluted, and with another "Guten Morgen, Excellenz!" left the train.

Turning to one of his companions, Von Moltke said, with an expression of the greatest disgust, "Intolerable gas-bag!"

* * * * *

A gentleman gave a large dinner party in Dublin once and invited Mr. O'Connor, one of the wittiest men in the Emerald Isle, to amuse and divert his guests. Mr. O'Connor accepted the invitation with pleasure. But from the beginning to the end of dinner he preserved a solemn and serious face. The host thought this very strange, and just before rising from the table remarked to him jestingly, "Why, O'Connor, old fellow, I don't believe the biggest fool in Ireland could make you laugh to-night." Whereupon his guest answered in a solemn tone, speaking his first word that evening, "Try."

* * * * *

Governor Guild of Massachusetts, who served in the Spanish War, tells a story of a New York regiment, many of whose members were recruited on the East Side. They were spoiling for a fight, and it became necessary to post a sentry to preserve order.

A big husky Bowery recruit, of pugilistic propensities, was put on guard outside, and given special orders to see that quiet reigned, and above all things, if trouble came his way, not to lose possession of his rifle.

Soon a general row began, growing in proportions as the minutes passed. The soldier walked his post nervously, without interrupting, until the corporal of the guard appeared on the scene with reenforcements.

"Why didn't you stop this row?" shouted the corporal.

The sentry, balancing his rifle on his shoulder, raised his arms to the correct boxing position, and replied:

"Sure, phwat could I do wid this gun in me hands!"

* * * * *

A New Jersey man recently reached the conclusion that his eight-year-old boy is a trifle too bright.

At dinner one evening the father had been entertaining a number of friends from Philadelphia with a funny story. This was at dessert. The youngster had been very quiet throughout the previous courses; but here he arose to the occasion in fine style.

When the laughter induced by his father's humor had ceased, the boy, with a fine affectation of delight, said:

"Now, dad, *do* tell the other one!"

* * * * *

The June bride frowned.

"These tomatoes," she said, "are just twice as dear as those across the street. Why is it?"

"Ah, ma'am, these"—and the grocer smiled—"these are hand-picked."

She blushed.

"Of course," she said, hastily; "I might have known. Give me a bushel, please."

* * * * *

Mistress—"Jane, I saw the milkman kiss you this morning. In the future I will take the milk in."

Jane—"'Twouldn't be no use, mum. He's promised never to kiss anybody but me."

* * * * *

Not long ago a man was charged with shooting a number of pigeons, the property of a farmer. In giving his evidence the farmer was exceedingly careful, even nervous, and the solicitor for the defense endeavored to frighten him. "Now," he remarked, "are you prepared to swear that this man shot your pigeons?" "I didn't say he did shoot 'em," was the reply. "I said I suspected him o' doing it." "Ah! now we're coming to it. What made you suspect that man?" "Well, firstly, I caught him on my land wi' a gun. Secondly, I heerd a gun go off an' saw some pigeons fall. Thirdly, I found four o' my pigeons in his pocket—an' I don't think them birds flew there and committed suicide."

* * * * *

"Mama, can't I go up to the next block and play with the Jones boys?" asked

Henry, a boy of six, who was being brought up very carefully.

"No, indeed!" answered his mother. "They are very bad boys."

"Then can't I go over to see Mrs. Smith's little girls?"

"No, Henry; I'm afraid to let you go."

The little fellow left the room; later, he stuck his head inside with, "Say, mama, I'm going over next door an' play with the dog."

* * * * *

The Right Reverend Chauncey B. Brewster, D.D., Bishop of Connecticut, tells a story which he says is Mrs. Brewster's favorite. It seems the Bishop had caught a small boy stealing apples in his orchard; so, after reproving him severely for some time, he said, "And now, my boy, do you know why I tell you all this? There is One before whom even I am a crawling worm; do you know who?"

"Sure," replied the boy, promptly; "the missus."

* * * * *

A Bishop was once traveling third-class on a branch line in Devonshire, England. At one of the stations a countryman got in. After gazing at the Bishop's attire in a puzzled manner for some time, he ventured the remark, "Be you a curate, sir?"

"Well," said the Bishop meditatively, "I was once."

"A-ah," said the rustic, a comprehensive smile overspreading his face, "the drink, I suppose?"

* * * * *

A celebrated parson preached a rather long sermon from the text "Thou art weighed and found wanting." After the congregation had listened about an hour, some began to get weary and went out; others soon followed, greatly to the annoyance of the minister. Another person was about to retire when the minister stopped his sermon and said: "That's right, gentlemen; as fast as you are weighed, pass out."

* * * * *

"Here, hold my horse a minute, will you?"

"Sir! I'm a Member of Congress!"

"Never mind. You look honest. I'll take a chance."

* * * * *

A red-faced man was holding the attention of a little group with some wonderful recitals.

"The most exciting chase I ever had," he said, "happened a few years ago in Russia. One night, when sleighing about ten miles from my destination I discovered, to my intense horror, that I was being followed by a pack of wolves. I fired blindly into the pack, killing one of the brutes, and to my delight saw the others stop to devour it. After doing this, however, they still came on. I kept on repeating the dose, with the same result, and each occasion gave me an opportunity to whip up my horse. Finally there was only one wolf left, yet on it came, with its fierce eyes glowing in anticipation of a good, hot supper."

Here the man who had been sitting in the corner burst forth into a fit of laughter.

"Why, man," said he, "by your way of reckoning that last wolf must have had the rest of the pack inside him!"

"Ah!" said the red-faced man without a tremor, "now I remember, it did wobble a bit."

* * * * *

Frederic Remington, the illustrator, fresh from a Western trip on which he had been making studies of Indians and cowpunchers and things outdoors, met an art editor who insisted upon dragging him up to an exhibition of very impressionistic pictures.

"You don't seem enthusiastic," remarked the editor as they were coming out. "Didn't you like them?"

Remington, remembering what he had been told as a boy, counted ten before replying. Then:

"Like 'em? Say! I've got two maiden aunts in New Rochelle that can *knit* better pictures than those!"

* * * * *

The wife of General S. was doing some shopping one morning recently when, coming out of a store, she noticed a small country wagon draw up to the curb. In it sat a woman whom the lady recognized as a former servant in the family who had lost her husband some two or three years before. The woman was clad in deep mourning which had an air of newness about it. Mrs. S. hastened to greet the woman. "How is this, Bridget. I hope you haven't met with any recent bereavement?"

"No, mem, not so racent—it's for poor Mike. I allus said *when* I could I would— and so I *am*!"

* * * * *

Those who know a certain Southern Senator will picture his ample proportions when they read this story:

While journeying through the South, he was very much annoyed one day at the delay in getting food served in a certain *café*. He had given his order, and waited impatiently an unreasonable length of time, when the waiter appeared and was evidently looking for some one who must have gone out without waiting for his meal.

When asked by the Senator whom he was looking for he replied.

"A little boy who gave his order."

The Senator replied: "I am that boy."

* * * * *

Jack's mother had been walking up and down the piazza with him repeating Mother Goose. She began the "Solomon Grundy" one, going through it rapidly without taking breath, ending laughingly:

"Worse on Friday,
Died on Saturday,
Buried on Sunday,
And that was the end
Of Solomon Grundy."

Jack took his thumb out of his mouth, looked reprovingly at his mother and said:

"Don't laugh, mama: that's *awful*."

* * * * *

"I'm a terror, I be," announced the new arrival in Frozen Dog to one of the men behind the bar.

"Be ye?"

"Take three men to handle me, once I get started," he went on.

* * * * *

"Oh, well," he remarked, as he arose painfully and dusted off his clothes, "of course, if ye're short-handed, I suppose two kin do it on a pinch."

* * * * *

David B. Hill, former Governor of and Senator from New York, has a secluded hatter somewhere in the State who makes his high hats after elaborate plans drawn by Mr. Hill many years ago, and not changed since.

One night Governor Odell, of New York, was giving a reception in Albany, and President Roosevelt, then elected Vice-President, met Mr. Hill on the steps of the New York Executive mansion.

Roosevelt wore a black rough-rider hat and Hill had one of his peculiar sky-pieces.

"Senator," said Roosevelt, "you should wear a hat like this one that I have on. They are much easier on the head, preserve the hair and are altogether better than silk ones."

Mr. Hill looked at the coming Vice-President. "My dear sir," he said, "I haven't worn a hat like that since I went out of the show business."

* * * * *

A negress was brought before a magistrate charged with cruelly treating her child. Evidence was clear that she had severely beaten the youngster, who was in court to exhibit his marks and bruises. Before imposing sentence the magistrate asked the woman if she had anything to say. "Kin Ah ask yo' honah a question?" His honor nodded. "Well, yo' honah, I'd like to ask yo' whether yo' was ever the father of a puffectly wuthless culled chile?"

* * * * *

A member of an eminent St. Louis law firm went to Chicago to consult a client. When he arrived he found that he had unaccountably forgotten the client's name. He telegraphed his partner, "What is our client's name?" The answer read, "Brown, Walter E. Yours is Allen, William B."

* * * * *

A traveling man stopped at an Indiana hotel. The proprietor told him he had not a room in the house. The man said he must have a room. Finally the proprietor told him there was a room, a little room separated by a thin partition from a nervous man who had lived in the house for ten years.

"He is so nervous," said the landlord, "I don't dare put any one in that room. The least noise might give him a nervous spell that would endanger his life."

"Oh, give me a room," said the traveler. "I'll be so quiet he'll not know I'm there."

The room was given the traveler. He slipped in noiselessly and began to disrobe. He took off one article of clothing after another as quietly as a burglar. At last he came to his shoes. He unlaced a shoe and dropped it.

The shoe fell to the floor with a great noise. The offending traveler, horrified at what he had done, waited to hear from the nervous man. Not a sound. He took off the second shoe and placed it noiselessly upon the floor; then in absolute silence finished undressing and crawled between the sheets.

Half an hour went by. He had dropped into a doze when there came a tremendous knocking on the partition.

The traveler sat up in bed trembling and dismayed. "Wh-wha-what's the matter?" he asked.

Then came the voice of the nervous man:

"Hang you! Drop that other shoe, will you?"

* * * * *

There was once an Irishman, who sought employment as a diver, bringing with him his native enthusiasm and a certain amount of experience. Although he had never been beneath the water, he had crossed an ocean of one variety and swallowed nearly an ocean of another. But he had the Hibernian smile, which is convincing, and the firm chanced to need a new man. And so on the following Monday morning Pat hid his smile for the first time in a diving helmet.

Now, the job upon which the crew to which Pat had attached himself was working in comparatively shallow water, and Pat was provided with a pick and told to use it on a ledge below in a manner with which he was already familiar.

Down he went with his pick, and for about fifteen minutes nothing was heard from him. Then came a strong, determined, deliberate pull on the signal rope, indicating that Pat had a very decided wish to come to the top. The assistants pulled him hastily to the raft and removed his helmet.

"Take off the rest of it," said Pat.

"Take off the rest of it?"

"Yis," said Pat, "Oi'll worruk no longer in a dark place where Oi can't spit on me hands."

* * * * *

On the first day that a young man began his duties as reporter on a popular paper a report came from a near-by town that there was a terrible fire raging. The editor of the paper immediately sent the new reporter to the place, and, upon arriving there, he found that the firemen were unable to get control of the fire, so he sent this telegram to the editor: "Fire still raging. What shall I do?" The editor was so mad that he wired back at once: "Find out where the fire is the hottest and jump in."

* * * * *

"One day," related Denny to his friend Jerry, "when Oi had wandered too far inland on me shore leave Oi suddenly found thot there was a great big haythen, tin feet tall, chasin' me wid a knife as long as yer ar-rm. Oi took to me heels an' for fifty miles along the road we had it nip an' tuck. Thin Oi turned into the woods an' we run for one hundhred an' twinty miles more, wid him gainin' on me steadily, owin' to his knowledge of the counthry. Finally, just as Oi could feel his hot breath burnin' on the back of me neck, we came to a big lake. Wid one great leap Oi landed safe on the opposite shore, leavin' me pursuer confounded and impotent wid rage."

"Faith an' thot was no great jump," commented Jerry, "considerin' the runnin' sthart ye had."

* * * * *

Quite recently an old friend of the Browns went to see them at their new country home. As he approached the house a large dog ran out to the gate and began barking at him through the fence.

As he hesitated about opening the gate, Brown's wife came to the door and exclaimed: "How do you do! Come right in. Don't mind the dog."

"But won't he bite?" exclaimed the friend, not anxious to meet the canine without some assurance of his personal safety.

"That's just what I want to find out," exclaimed Mrs. Brown. "I just bought him this morning."

* * * * *

The late Julian Ralph, one of the most gifted newspaper men of his generation, while being shaved one day, was forced to listen to many of the barber's anecdotes.

Stopping to strop his razor, and prepared, with brush in hand to recommence, he said, "Shall I go over it again?"

"No, thanks," drawled Ralph, "It's hardly necessary. I think I can remember every word."

* * * * *

The following is a typical Ian Maclaren story:

"Who had this place last year?" asked a Southern shooting tenant of his keeper.

"Well," said Donald, "I'm not denyin' that he wass an Englishman, but he wass a good man whatever. Oh, yess, he went to kirk and he shot very well, but he wass narrow, very narrow."

"Narrow," said the other in amazement, for he supposed he meant bigoted, and the charge was generally the other way about. "What was he narrow in?"

"Well," said Donald, "I will be tellin' you, and it wass this way. The twelfth [the beginning of the grouse shooting] wass a very good day, and we had fifty-two brace. But it wass warm, oh! yess, very warm, and when we came back to the Lodge, the gentleman will say to me, 'It is warm.' and I will not be contradicting him. Then he will be saying, 'Maybe you are thirsty,' and I will not be contradicting him. Afterwards he will take out his flask and be speaking about a dram. I will not be contradicting him, but will just say, 'Toots, toots.' Then he will be pouring it out, and when the glass wass maybe half-full I will say, just for politeness, 'Stop.' And he stopped. Oh! yess, a very narrow man."

* * * * *

Mark Twain as a humorist is no respecter of persons, and a story is told of him and Bishop Doane which is worth repeating. It occurred when Mark Twain was living in Hartford, where Mr. Doane was then rector of an Episcopal church. Twain had listened to one of the doctor's best sermons, on Sunday morning, when he approached him and said politely: "I have enjoyed your sermon this morning. I welcomed it as I would an old friend. I have a book in my library that contains every word of it." "Impossible, sir," replied the rector, indignantly. "Not at all. I assure you it is true," said Twain. "Then I shall trouble you to send me that book," rejoined the rector with dignity. The next morning Dr. Doane received, with Mark Twain's compliments, a dictionary.

* * * * *

A friend of Mark Twain's tells of an amusing incident in connection with the first meeting between the humorist and the late James McNeil Whistler, the artist.

The friend having facetiously warned Clemens that the painter was a confirmed joker, Mark solemnly averred that he would get the better of Whistler should the latter attempt "any funny business." Furthermore, Twain determined to anticipate Whistler, if possible.

So, when the two had been introduced, which event took place in Whistler's studio, Clemens, assuming an air of hopeless stupidity, approached a just-completed painting, and said:

"Not at all bad, Mr. Whistler, not at all bad. Only," he added, reflectively, with a motion as if to rub out a cloud effect, "if I were you I'd do away with that cloud."

"Great Heavens, sir!" exclaimed Whistler, almost beside himself. "Do be careful not to touch that; the paint is not yet dry!"

"Oh, I don't mind that," responded Twain, with an air of perfect nonchalance; "I am wearing gloves."

* * * * *

This is a story of Italian revenge. A vender of plaster statuettes saw a chance for a sale in a well-dressed, bibulous man who was tacking down the street.

"You buy-a de statuette?" he asked, alluringly holding out his choicest offering. "Gar-r-ribaldi—I sell-a him verra cheep. De gr-reat-a Gar-r-ribaldi—only thirta cents!"

"Oh, t'ell with Garibaldi," said the bibulous one, making a swipe with his arm that sent Garibaldi crashing to the sidewalk.

For a moment the Italian regarded the fragments. Then, his eyes flashing fire, he seized from his stock a statuette of George Washington. "You t'ell-a with my Gar-r-ribaldi?" he hissed between his teeth. "So." He raised the immortal George high above his head and—crash! it flew into fragments alongside of the ill-fated Garibaldi. "Ha! I to hell-a wid your George-a Wash! Ha, ha!"

* * * * *

Patrick arrived home much the worse for wear. One eye was closed, his nose was broken, and his face looked as though it had been stung by bees.

"Glory be!" exclaimed his wife.

"Thot Dutchman Schwartzheimer—'twas him," explained Patrick.

"Shame on ye!" exploded his wife without sympathy. "A big shpalpeen the loikes of you to get bate up by a little omadhoun of a Dootchman the size of him! Why—"

"Whist, Nora," said Patrick, "don't spake disrespectfully of the dead!"

* * * * *

One day a teacher in a kindergarten school in New York, preparatory to giving out an exercise said, "Now children I want you all to be very quiet, so quiet that you could hear a pin drop." Everything had quieted down nicely and the teacher was about to speak when a little voice in the rear of the room said, "Go ahead, teacher, and let her drop."

* * * * *

It appears that the late Senator John T. Morgan, who was quite near-sighted, while at dessert one evening in a hotel at Hot Springs, Virginia, experienced considerable difficulty in separating from the plate passed him by the colored waiter what he thought was a chocolate eclair. It stuck fast, so Senator Morgan pushed his fork quite under it, and tried again and again to pry it up.

Suddenly he became aware that his friends at the table were convulsed with laughter, which much mystified him. But his surprise was even greater when the waiter quietly remarked:

"Pardon me, Senator, but that's my thumb!"

* * * * *

A doctor named Brown had been the adorer for many years of a Miss White. Unluckily his ardent love was not reciprocated. He had a reputation for ready wit and did not allow even his unfortunate love affair to stand in the way of his exercising it. One night over a glass of wine in the club the good doctor frequented a wag remarked, "What do you say, doctor, to my giving the toast of Miss White, your old flame?" "You may, and you'll not do any harm either to her or to me by toasting her as often as you please, for I've toasted her all these years and there are still no symptoms of her turning Brown."

* * * * *

Minister (who struggles to exist on $600 a year with wife and six children)—"We are giving up meat as a little experiment, Mrs. Dasher."

Wealthy parishioner—"Oh, yes! One can live so well on fish, poultry, game, and plenty of nourishing wines."

* * * * *

A woman who traveled a great deal in the West was known as the most inveterate "kicker" a certain hotel had ever known.

One evening after she had been served with dessert this lady, who was always complaining, asked the waiter why the dish served her was called "ice-cream pudding."

"If you don't like it, ma'am, I'll bring you something else," suggested the polite negro.

"Oh, it's very nice," responded the lady. "What I object to is that it should be called ice-cream pudding. It's wrongly named. There should be ice cream served with it."

"Yes, ma'am," replied the waiter, "but that's jest our name for it. Lots o' dishes that way. Dey don't bring you a cottage with cottage pudding, you know."

* * * * *

During a certain cruise the first mate of a ship got to drinking to excess and was intoxicated for several days. One day, after having come out of this state, he examined the log book to see what had passed during his period of semi-forgetfulness. He was horrified to find entered in the book for the three days consecutively, "The first mate is drunk to-day." He did not want this to stand as it would hardly be a good recommendation for him to the ship owners and asked the captain to remove the entries.

The captain replied, "It is the truth, is it not?" "Yes, but—" replied the mate. The captain interrupted him, "If it is the truth, the truth must stand. It is written in ink and can not be removed without injuring the book."

A short time afterward the captain was taken ill and remained so for a week, and it devolved upon the mate to keep the log book. The captain on recovering from his illness got the book to examine it to see how the mate had done his duty. Imagine his consternation when he read in each of the seven days' entries, "The captain is sober to-day."

The captain immediately called the mate and indignantly questioned him in regard to these entries. The mate replied, "It is the truth, is it not?" "Yes, but—" replied the captain. The mate interrupted him, "If it is the truth, the truth must stand, must it not? I have your word that the writing in ink can not be erased."

* * * * *

"It was the first week of his honeymoon," said the hotel barber, "and he came in and sat down near the door to wait his turn. I yelled 'Next' at him two or three times when my chair was vacant, but he was dreaming and didn't hear me. Finally I touched him on the shoulder and told him I was ready for him.

"'What do you want me to do?' he asked.

"'Why, get in the chair if you want anything,' I replied. 'This is a barber shop.'

"'Oh, yes,' he said, and then he got into the chair. He leaned back, so I let the chair down and shaved him. He didn't have a word to say. When I finished him up he got out of the chair and took the check over to the cashier. He paid and started out. When halfway through the door he stopped.

"'Say,' he said to me, 'what did you do to me?'

"'I shaved you,' I said.

"'Darn the luck,' he replied, 'I wanted a haircut.'"

* * * * *

The little daughter of a homeopathic physician received a ring with a pearl in it on the Christmas tree. Two days later she poked her head tearfully in at the door of her father's office.

"Papa," she sobbed, "Papa, I've lost the little pill out of my ring."

* * * * *

He was from Pittsburg, Pa., and was stopping at the Manhattan Hotel. He wanted to telephone to a town about thirty miles away. He asked the girl on the switchboard to get him long-distance, and followed it up with asking the price.

"It will cost you 50 cents for three minutes," she said sweetly.

"Fifty cents! Ye gods!" cried the man. "I don't want to buy stock in the telephone company. I only want to talk a minute or so. Why—why—out in Pittsburg we can call up all Hades for 50 cents!"

"Yes, I know, sir," replied the girl, "but isn't that within your city limits?"

* * * * *

General St. Clair Mulholland, veteran and historian of the civil war, tells an incident showing the utter worthlessness of Confederate paper money at the close of the war. "Shortly after Lee's surrender," says the General, "I was a short distance from Richmond. The Confederate soldiers were going home to become men of peace again and were thinking about their farms. One had a lame, broken-down horse which he viewed with pride. 'Wish I had him, Jim,' said the other. 'What'll you take for him? I'll give you $20,000 for him.' 'No,' said Jim. 'Give you $50,000.' 'No,' said Jim. 'Give you $100,000,' his friend said. 'Not much,' replied Jim, 'I just gave $120,000 to have him shod.'"

* * * * *

The Magistrate—"You seem to have committed a very grave assault on the defendant just because he differed from you in an argument."

The Defendant—"There was no help for it, your worship. The man is a perfect idiot."

The Magistrate—"Well, you must pay a fine of 50 francs and costs, and in future you should try and understand that idiots are human beings, the same as you and I."

* * * * *

Sentimental Young Lady—"Ah Professor! what would this old oak say if it could talk?"

Professor—"It would say, 'I am an elm.'"

* * * * *

"You needn't begin jollying me," said the gruff man to the man who had land to sell. "I'm not a man that can be affected by flattery. When I—"

"That's just what I said to my boss," interrupted the agent. "I told him, when he suggested your name to me, that it was a relief to call on a man who did not expect to be praised and flattered to his face all the time. I tell you, Mr. Grump, this city has mighty few men such as you. Nine men out of ten are simply dying to have some one tell them how great they are, but you are above such weakness. Any one can see that at a glance. I'm glad of it. It's helpful to me to meet a man who rises superior to the petty tactics of the average solicitor. It's a real and lasting benefit, and an instructive experience."

Ten minutes later, after a few more such comments on the part of the agent, the man who could not be flattered into signing the contract was asking which line his name should be written upon.

* * * * *

Billy Martin, aged four, came to his mother and in great ecstasy exclaimed, "Oh, mother! Louise and Carberry found such a nice dead cat, and they are going to have a funeral, and can I go?" Permission was given, and when Billy returned he was questioned as to the outcome of the funeral.

"They did not have it at all."

"And why not?"

"Mother," was the answer, "the cat was too dead."

* * * * *

The late H. C. Bunner when editor of "Puck," once received a letter accompanying a number of would-be jokes in which the writer asked: "What will you give me for these?" "Ten yards start," was Bunner's generous offer, written beneath the query.

* * * * *

One day Riley was riding on top of a 'bus in London with his friend Casey. He was nearly worn out with several hours' sight-seeing and the bustle and excitement of the London street, the hoi polloi, the Billingsgate and the din and rattle were becoming almost unbearable when they came in sight of Westminster Abbey. Just as they did so, the chimes burst forth in joyous melody, and he said to Casey, "Isn't it sublime? Isn't it glorious to hear those chimes pealing and doesn't it inspire one with renewed vigor?" Casey leaned over, with hand to his ear, and said, "You'll have to speak a little louder, Riley; I can't hear you." Riley continued, "Those magnificent chimes. Do you not hear them pealing? Do they not imbue you with a feeling of almost reverence? Do they not awaken tender memories of the past?" Casey again leaned forward and said, "I can't hear you. You'll have to speak louder." Riley got as close to him as possible and said, "Do you not hear the melodious pealing of the chimes? Do they not recall the salutation of old Trinity on a Sabbath morning? Do they not take you back into the dim vistas of the past when the world was young, and touch your heart with a feeling of pathos?" Casey put his mouth close to Riley's ear and said, "Those d— bells are making such a racket, Riley, that I can't hear you."

* * * * *

Four grinning urchins sat on the street curb eulogizing ex-President Roosevelt.

"Say, dat guy Roosevelt 'll fight at de drop of de hat!" declared one youngster. "I read dat durin' a talk at de White House one of de party said somethin' the President wouldn' stan' for an' he leans over an gets de guy's ear!"

* * * * *

"Have you ever had any experience in canvassing for subscription books?" asked the man at the desk.

"No, sir," said the applicant for a job, "but I can put up a good talk."

"Well, take a copy of this work and go and see if you can get an order. I'll give you half a day to make the trial."

The applicant went away.

In an hour or two he returned.

"What luck?" inquired the man at the desk.

"I've got an order for this book in full morocco from your wife, sir."

"You'll do, young man."

* * * * *

In Alabama they tell this story to illustrate Senator Morgan's ability as an advocate. A negro of well-known thieving proclivities was on trial for stealing a mule. Morgan defended and cleared him. As lawyer and client were walking out of the courtroom Mr. Morgan said: "Rastus, did you steal the mule?" "Well, Marse Morgan, it was jes like dis: I really thought I did steal dat mule, but after what you said to the jury I was convince' I didn't."

* * * * *

Uncle Walter, with his little niece Ruth in his lap, was about to telephone a message to a distant city. While waiting for the connection to be made little Ruth asked if she might talk over the open wire. The young lady operator heard the question and said, "Yes, please let her."

Ruth, taking the receiver, first told her name. Then the operator asked her where she was, and to this Ruth replied:

"I am in Uncle Walter's lap—don't you wish you were?"

* * * * *

Apropos of vanity, Senator Root told at Yale about a politician who, the day before he was to make a certain speech, sent a forty-one-page report of it to all the papers. On page 20 appeared this paragraph: "But the hour grows late, and I must close. (No, no! Go on! Go on!)"

* * * * *

Two women from the country were at the circus for the first time. They were greatly taken with the menagerie. At last they came to the hippopotamus, and stood for several minutes in silent wonder, then one turned to the other and said, "My, Mandy, ain't—he—*plain*?"

* * * * *

Senator Ingalls was always quick at retort, although he was himself a subject of some sharp shafts. Once he was attacked by Senator Eli Saulsbury, of Delaware, the second smallest State in the Union. He disposed of the whole matter by saying, "I thank the gentleman from that great State, which has three counties at low tide and two counties at high tide, for his advice."

* * * * *

A young and bashful professor was frequently embarrassed by jokes his girl pupils would play on him. These jokes were so frequent that he decided to punish the next perpetrators, and the result of this decision was that two girls were detained an hour after school, and made to work some difficult problems, as punishment.

It was the custom to answer the roll-call with quotations, so the following morning, when Miss A's name was called, she rose, and, looking straight in the professor's eye, repeated: "With all thy faults I love thee still," while Miss B's quotation was: "The hours I spend with thee, dear heart, are as a string of pearls to me."

* * * * *

Archbishop Patrick J. Ryan, of Philadelphia, once received a call from Wayne McVeagh, in company with Mr. Roberts, president of the Pennsylvania system at the time that McVeagh was counsel for that railroad. "Your Grace," said Mr. McVeagh, "Mr. Roberts, who always travels with his counsel, will, undoubtedly, get you passes over all the railroads in the United States, if in return you will get him a pass to Paradise." "I would do so gladly," flashed the archbishop, "if it were not for separating him from his counsel."

* * * * *

On one of his collecting trips through Scotland the eminent English geologist, Hugh Miller, at the end of the day gave to a servant his bag of specimen stones which he had labored all day to collect, to be carried some miles to his home. Later, while sitting unobserved in a corner of the village inn, he heard the man communicating to a friend in Gaelic his experience with the "mad Englishman," as he called him, in the following manner:

"He gave me his bag to carry home by a short-cut across the hills while he walked by another road. I was wondering why it was so fearfully heavy, and when I got out of his sight I made up my mind to see what was in it. I opened it, and what do you think it was? Stones!"

"Stones!" exclaimed his companion, opening his eyes. "Stones! Well, that beats all I ever heard or knew of one of them. And did you carry it?"

"Carry it! Do you think I was as mad as himself? No, no. I emptied them all out of the bag, but I filled it again from the stone-heap near the house, and gave him good measure for his money."

* * * * *

Former Representative Gibson, of Tennessee, had a voice that would play tricks with him. It would work all right for a few minutes, and then it would stop entirely, and Gibson would be left gasping for a moment or two, high and dry in the middle of his argument, until his voice came back again. He was making a tariff speech one day, sailing along in fine shape. "Why, Mr. Speaker," he shouted, "the tariff is like a pair of suspenders. Uncle Sam needs it to keep up his—"

Right there his voice broke. Gibson couldn't say a word.

"Trousers!" yelled one member.

"Pants!"

"Breeches!"

By that time the voice came back—"to keep up his revenues," said Gibson, glaring around at his tormentors.

* * * * *

Senator Tillman not long ago piloted a plain farmer-constituent around the Capitol for a while, and then, having some work to do on the floor, conducted him to the Senate gallery.

After an hour or so the visitor approached a gallery doorkeeper and said: "My name is Swate. I am a friend of Senator Tillman. He brought me here and I want to go out and look around a bit. I thought I would tell you so I can get back in."

"That's all right," said the doorkeeper, "but I may not be here when you return. In order to prevent any mistake I will give you the password so you can get your seat again."

Swate's eyes rather popped out at this. "What's the word?" he asked.

"Idiosyncrasy."

"What?"

"Idiosyncrasy."

"I guess I'll stay in," said Swate.

* * * * *

The Willoughbys had said good-by to Mrs. Kent. Then Mr. Willoughby spoke thoughtfully:

"It was pleasant of her to say that about wishing she could see more of people like us, who are interested in real things, instead of the foolish round of gaiety that takes up so much of her time and gives her so little satisfaction, wasn't it?"

His wife stole a sidewise glance at his gratified face and a satirical smile crossed her own countenance.

"Very pleasant, George," she said clearly. "But what I knew she meant, and what she knew that I knew she meant, was that my walking-skirt is an inch too long and my sleeves are old style, and your coat, poor dear, is beginning to look shiny in the back."

"Why—what—how—" began Mr. Willoughby helplessly; then he shook his head and gave it up.

* * * * *

Mrs. Wharton, the novelist, has never described any blunder of the so-called smart set quite as pathetic as one that actually happened to herself. A young man of a particularly old family, who sat next to her at dinner, said: "I'm terribly frightened to meet you, Mrs. Wharton," and when asked the origin of his terrors, explained: "I've always heard you're such a frightful blackleg."

* * * * *

Rosenthal, the pianist, speaks eight or ten languages. But his knowledge of idiomatic English has not always been sufficient to enable him to follow all the critics have said about his pyrotechnic playing. The other day, reading over the latest batch of clippings in the manager's office, he suddenly asked: "Vat iss 'Fourt' of July interpretation?"

"Fourth of July?" was the reply, "Don't you know the Fourth of July? Why, the national holiday—everything noble and patriotic—George Washington—Battle of Bunker Hill—the Declaration of Independence—" "Ah! I see," said the pianist, "Un grand compliment!"

* * * * *

Representative Cushman, of Washington, once came to Speaker Cannon with a letter written by the speaker himself.

"Mr. Speaker," he said, "I got this letter from you yesterday and I couldn't read it. I showed it to twenty or thirty fellows in the House and, between us, we have spelled out all but the last three words." Uncle Joe took the letter and studied it, "The last three words," he said, "are 'Personal and Confidential.'"

* * * * *

At a banquet held in a room the walls of which were adorned with many beautiful paintings, a well-known college president was called upon to respond to a toast. In the course of his remarks, wishing to pay a compliment to the ladies present, and designating the paintings with one of his characteristic gestures, he said: "What need is there of these painted beauties when we have so many with us at this table?"

* * * * *

The late Charles Eliot Norton was wont to deplore the modern youth's preference of brawn to brain. He used to tell of a football game he once witnessed: "Princeton had a splendid player in Poe—you will remember little Poe?" and Professor Norton, thinking of "The Raven" and "Annabel Lee," said to the lad at his side: "He plays well, that Poe!"

"Doesn't he?" the youth cried. "Is he," said Professor Norton, "any relation to the great Poe?"

"Any relation?" said the youth. "Why, he is the great Poe."

* * * * *

A fire broke out one day in Francis Wilson's dressing-room at the theater where he was playing.

He had some of his books around him, and in an agony of despair asked himself:

"Which shall I save?" He glanced at his precious Chaucer, at some Shakespearean volumes, when:

"Come, Mr. Wilson," broke in at the door from a fireman, "you have not a moment to lose."

"Yes, yes. Coming," replied Wilson absently.

He was looking for a special illuminated volume very dear to him.

"Come, Wilson," cried his manager; "come, get out!"

"All right, all right," said Wilson, and, grabbing some clothes in one hand, he snatched with the other the nearest volume and ran to the street. There he looked at the huge volume in his arms. It was the city directory.

* * * * *

A city gentleman was recently invited down to the country for "a day with the birds." His aim was not remarkable for its accuracy, to the great disgust of the man in attendance, whose tip was generally regulated by the size of the bag.

"Dear me!" at last exclaimed the sportsman, "but the birds seem exceptionally strong on the wing this year."

"Not all of 'em, sir," was the answer. "You've shot at the same bird about a dozen times. 'E's a-follerin' you about, sir."

"Following me about? Nonsense! Why should a bird do that?"

"Well, sir," came the reply. "I dunno, I'm sure, unless 'e's 'angin' 'round you for safety."

* * * * *

A lady was calling on some friends one summer afternoon. The talk buzzed along briskly, fans waved and the daughter of the house kept twitching uncomfortably, frowning and making little smothered exclamations of annoyance. Finally, with a sigh, she rose and left the room.

"Your daughter," said the visitor, "seems to be suffering from the heat."

"No," said the hostess. "She is just back home from college and she is suffering from the family grammar."

* * * * *

"It ain't everybody I'd put to sleep in this room," said old Mrs. Jinks to the fastidious and extremely nervous young minister who was spending a night at her house.

"This here room is full of sacred associations to me," she went on, as she bustled around opening shutters and arranging the curtains. "My first husband died in that bed with his head on these very pillers, and poor Mr. Jinks died settin' right in that corner. Sometimes when I come into the room in the dark I think I see him settin' there still.

"My own father died layin' right on that lounge under the winder. Poor pa! He was a Speeritualist, and he allus said he'd appear in this room after he died, and sometimes I'm foolish enough to look for him. If you should see anything of him to-night you'd better not tell me; for it'd be a sign to me that there was something in Speeritualism, and I'd hate to think that.

"My son by my first man fell dead of heart disease right where you stand. He was a doctor, and there's two skeletons in that closet that belonged to him, and half a dozen skulls in that lower drawer.

"There, I guess you'll be comfortable.

"Well, good night, and pleasant dreams."

* * * * *

A woman suffrage lecturer brought down the house with the following argument: "I have no vote, but my groom has, but I am sure if I were to go to him and say, 'John, will you exercise the franchise?' he would reply, 'Please, mum, which horse be that?'"

* * * * *

"Maude was afraid the girls wouldn't notice her engagement ring." "Did they?" "*Did* they? Six of them recognized it at once."

* * * * *

Mr. George Broadhurst, author of the play, "The Man of the Hour," is an Englishman, and recently made a visit to his native country. After having lived a week at one of the large hotels in London, he was surprised on the evening of his departure, although at a very late hour, to see an endless procession of waiters, maids, porters, and pages come forward with the expectant smile and empty hand. When each and all had been well bestowed, even boots and under-boots and then another boots, he dashed for the four-wheeler that was to carry him safely away.

Settling himself with a sigh of relief, he was about to be off when a page popped his head into the window and breathlessly exclaimed:

"I beg pardon, sir, but the night-lift man says he's waiting for a message from you, sir."

"A message from me?"

"Yes, sir; he says he cawn't go to sleep without a message from you, sir."

"Really, he can't go to sleep without a message from me?"

"No, sir."

"How touching. Then tell him, 'Pleasant dreams.'"

* * * * *

Representative Tawney, of Minnesota, chairman of the House Committee on Appropriations, sent out some of his quota of garden seeds to his constituents not long ago. One man in Winona wrote to Tawney: "Dear Jim: I received your seeds, but I don't care much for them. If you really want to do something for me, please send me up a suit of union underwear."

* * * * *

In his younger days Thomas Bailey Aldrich was not a little of a dandy. This foible led an unusually energetic Boston bluestocking to refer to him in a caustic style on one occasion as "effeminate."

When a friend told the poet of her remark he smiled grimly.

"So I am," he assented, "compared with her."

* * * * *

Tennyson's customary manner toward women was one of grave and stately courtesy. One evening at Aldworth, Sir Edward Hamley, the soldier and expert writer on the art of war, who had been visiting through the day, rose to take leave. Tennyson pressed him to stay over night, adding: "There are three ladies who wish it," meaning Mrs. Tennyson and the two guests who were in the house.

"There are three other ladies who oppose it," Sir Edward answered.

"Who are they?" Tennyson asked.

"The Fates," Sir Edward replied.

"The Fates may be on one side," Tennyson rejoined, "but the Graces are on the other."

* * * * *

Douglas Jerrold's genius for repartee is perhaps best shown in his most famous reply to Albert Smith, whom he disliked and frequently abused. Smith grew tired of being made the butt of the other's wit, and one day plaintively remarked: "After all, Jerrold, we row in the same boat." "Yes," came the answer, "but not with the same skulls."

* * * * *

Mr. Brown, a Kansas gentleman, is the proprietor of a boarding-house. Around his table at a recent dinner sat his wife, Mrs. Brown; the village milliner, Mrs. Andrews; Mr. Black, the baker; Mr. Jordan, a carpenter; and Mr. Hadley, a flour, feed, and lumber merchant. Mr. Brown took a ten-dollar bill out of his pocketbook and handed it to Mrs. Brown, with the remark that there was ten dollars toward the twenty he had promised her. Mrs. Brown handed the bill to Mrs. Andrews, the milliner, saying, "That pays for my new bonnet." Mrs. Andrews, in turn, passed it on to Mr. Jordan, remarking that it would pay for the carpentry work he had done for her. Mr. Jordan handed it to Mr. Hadley, requesting his receipted bill for flour, feed, and lumber. Mr. Hadley gave the bill back to Mr. Brown, saying, "That pays ten dollars on my board." Mr. Brown again passed it to Mrs. Brown, remarking that he had now paid her the twenty dollars he had promised her. She, in turn, paid it to Mr. Black to settle her bread and pastry account. Mr. Black handed it to Mr. Hadley, asking credit for the amount on his flour bill, Mr. Hadley again returning it to Mr. Brown, with the remark that it settled for that month's board; whereupon Brown put it back into his pocketbook, observing that he had not supposed a greenback would go so far.

* * * * *

A doctor came up to a patient in an insane asylum, slapped him on the back, and said: "Well, old man, you're all right, you can run along and write your folks that you'll be back home in two weeks as good as new." The patient went off gaily to write his letter. He had it finished and sealed, but when he was licking the stamp it slipped through his fingers to the floor, lighted on the back of a cockroach that was passing and stuck. The patient hadn't seen the cockroach — what he did see was his escaped postage stamp zig-zagging aimlessly across the floor to the baseboard, wavering up over the baseboard and following a crooked track up the wall and across the ceiling. In depressed silence he tore up the letter and dropped the pieces on the floor. "Two weeks! Hell!" he said. "I won't be out of here in three years."

* * * * *

A Bostonian, arriving at the gate of Heaven, asked for admittance.

"Where are you from?" inquired the genial Saint.

"Boston."

"Well, you can come in, but you won't like it."

* * * * *

A well-known bishop, after a long journey to conduct a service in a distant village, was asked by the spokesman of the reception committee if he would like a whisky and soda to keep out the cold. "No," he replied, "for three reasons. First, because I am chairman of the Temperance Society; secondly, I am just going to enter a church; and—thirdly, because—I have just had one."

* * * * *

A frivolous young English girl, with no love for the Stars and Stripes, once exclaimed at a celebration where the American flag was very much in evidence: "Oh, what a silly-looking thing the American flag is! It suggests nothing but checker-berry candy."

"Yes," replied a bystander, "the kind of candy that has made everybody sick who ever tried to lick it."

* * * * *

A hungry Irishman went into a restaurant on Friday and said to the waiter:

"Have yez any whale?"

"No."

"Have yez any shark?"

"No."

"Have yez any swordfish?"

"No."

"Have yez any jellyfish?"

"No."

"All right," said the Irishman. "Then bring me ham and eggs and a beefsteak smothered wid onions. The Lord knows I asked for fish."

* * * * *

Mr. Halloran returned from a political meeting with his interest aroused. "There's eight nations represented in this ward of ours," he said, as he began to count them off on his fingers. "There's Irish, Frinch, Eyetalians, Poles, Germans, Rooshians, Greeks, an'—" Mr. Halloran stopped and began again: "There's Irish,

Frinch, Eyetalians, Poles, Germans, Rooshians, Greeks, an'—I can't seem to re-member the other wan. There's Irish, Frinch—" "Maybe 'twas Americans," sug-gested Mrs. Halloran. "Sure, that's it, I couldn't think."

*****

The solemnity of the meeting was somewhat disturbed when the eloquent young theologian pictured in glowing words the selfishness of men who spend their evenings at the club, leaving their wives in loneliness at home at the holiday season. "Think, my hearers," said he, "of a poor, neglected wife, all alone in the great, dreary house, rocking the cradle of her sleeping babe with one foot and wiping away her tears with the other!"

*****

Two charming girls with Mr. Danvers, who was very shy, were watching the dancing waves. Conversation was carried on with difficulty. Finally Maude ven-tured the remark:

"Don't you hate the seaside, Mr. Danvers, with its glare and noise and general vulgarity?"

Mr. Danvers replied fervently with a smile and downcast eyes: "Oh, d-d-d-don't I, that's all!"

Then Miss Lilian followed up the subject and said: "What, hate the seaside, Mr. Danvers?—with the fresh air and blue waves, and the delightful lounge after bathing, and the lawn-tennis and the Cinderella dances! I dote on it, and I should have thought you did, too!"

Whereupon Mr. Danvers stammered still more fervently: "Oh—I-I-I should think I did!"

And the waves kept on splashing merrily.

*****

Just before the collection was taken up one Sunday morning a negro clergy-man announced that he regretted to state that a certain brother had forgotten to lock the door of his chicken-house the night before, and as a result in the morning he found that most of the fowls had disappeared. "I doan' want to be pussonal, bredr'n," he added, "but I hab my s'picions as to who stole dem chickens. I also hab reason fo' b'lievin' dat if I am right in dose s'picions dat pusson won't put any money in de plate which will now be passed around."

The result was a fine collection; not a single member of the congregation feigned sleep. After it was counted the old parson came forward.

"Now, bredr'n," he said, "I doan' want your dinners to be spoilt by wonderin' where dat brudder lives who doan' lock his chickens up at night. Dat brudder doan' exist, mah friends. He was a parable gotten up fo' purpose of finances."

*****

A minister in a Western town was called upon one afternoon to perform the marriage ceremony between a negro couple—the negro preacher of the town being absent from home.

After the ceremony the groom asked the price of the service.

"Oh, well," said the minister, "you can pay me whatever you think it is worth to you."

The negro turned and silently looked his bride over from head to foot, then slowly rolling up the whites of his eyes, said:

"Lawd, sah, you has done ruined me for life, you has, for shuah."

* * * * *

A professor of sciences, well known for his absent-mindedness, was engaged in a deep controversy one day with a fellow-student when his wife hurriedly entered the room. "Oh, my dear," she cried, "I've swallowed a pin."

The Professor smiled. "Don't worry about it, my dear," he said in a soothing tone. "It is of no consequence. Here"—he fumbled at his lapel—"Here is another pin."

* * * * *

The late Theodore Thomas was rehearsing the Chicago Orchestra on the stage of the Auditorium Theater. He was disturbed by the whistling of Burridge, the well-known scene painter, who was at work in the loft above the stage. A few minutes later Mr. Thomas's librarian appeared on the "bridge," where Mr. Burridge, merrily whistling, was at work. "Mr. Thomas's compliments," said the librarian, "and he requests me to say that if Mr. Burridge wishes to whistle he will be glad to discontinue his rehearsal." To which Mr. Burridge replied suavely: "Mr. Burridge's compliments to Mr. Thomas; and please inform Mr. Thomas that, if Mr. Burridge can not whistle with the orchestra, he won't whistle at all."

* * * * *

When trouble was more general and more destructive in Ireland than at present, an Irish priest, a very good man, was disturbed by the inroads which strong drink was making on his flock. He preached a strong sermon against it. "What is it," he cried, "that keeps you poor? It's the drink. What is it keeps your children half-starved? The drink. What is it keeps your children half-clothed? The drink! The drink. What is it causes you to shoot at your landlords—and miss them? The drink."

* * * * *

Goff, the famous London barrister, has a humor peculiarly his own. He looks at the world in a half-amused, half-indulgent manner sometimes very annoying to his friends. One day, when in town, he dropped into a restaurant for lunch. It was a tidy, although not a pretentious establishment. After a good meal he called to the waitress and inquired what kind of pie could be had.

"Apple pie mince pie raisin pie blueberry pie custard pie peach pie and strawberry shortcake," the young woman repeated glibly.

"Will you please say that again?" he asked, leaning a trifle forward.

The girl went through the list at lightning rate. "And strawberry shortcake," she concluded with emphasis.

"Would you mind doing it once more?" he said.

The waitress looked her disgust, and started in a third time pronouncing the words in a defiantly clear tone.

"Thank you," he remarked when she had finished. "For the life of me I can not see how you do it. But I like to hear it. It's very interesting, very. Give me apple pie, please, and thank you very much."

* * * * *

An elderly Bishop, a bachelor, who was very fastidious about his toilet, was especially fond of his bath, and requested particular care of his tub from the maid.

When about to leave town one day he gave strict orders to the housemaid about his "bawth-tub" and said that no one was to be allowed the use of it.

Alas! the temptation grew on the girl and she took a plunge.

The Bishop returned unexpectedly, and finding traces of the recent stolen bath, questioned the maid so closely that she had to confess she was the culprit, and was very sorry.

"I hope you do not think it a sin, Bishop?" asked Mary in tears.

Eying her sternly, he said: "Mary your using my tub is not a sin, but what distresses me most is that you would do anything behind my back that you would not do before my face."

* * * * *

Senator Dawes, in his young manhood, was a very poor speaker. One time he was in an important law case, and for his opponent he had an older attorney whose eloquence attracted a crowd that packed the courtroom.

The day was very hot and the judge on the bench was freely perspiring. Finally the judge, drawing off his coat in the midst of the lawyer's eloquent address, said:

"Mr. Attorney, excuse me, but suppose you sit down and let Dawes begin to speak. I want to thin out this crowd."

* * * * *

A doctor spending a rare and somewhat dull night at his own fireside received the following message from three fellow practitioners:

"Please step over to the club and join us at a rubber of whist."

"Jane, dear," he said to his wife, "I am called away again. It appears to be a difficult case—there are three other doctors on the spot already."

* * * * *

George, the four-year-old grandson of an extremely pious and devout grandfather, came rushing into the house in a state of wild excitement. "Grandpa! Grandpa!" he called. "Mr. Barton's cow is dead! God called her home!"

*****

Philander C. Knox tells this story of Roosevelt: "Roosevelt," he said, "was surprised by a Kansas delegation at Oyster Bay one summer. The President appeared with his coat and collar off, trousers hitched by belt, and mopping his forehead. 'Ah, gentlemen,' he said, '*de*lighted to see you, *de*lighted. But I am very busy putting in my hay, you know. Just come down to the barn with me and we'll talk it over while I work.' Down to the barn hustled the delegation and Mr. Roosevelt seized a pitchfork. But, behold there was no hay on the floor! 'John,' shouted the President to sounds in the hayloft; 'where's all the hay?' 'I ain't had time to throw it back since you threw it up yesterday, sir.'"

*****

Before the President of a certain Western college had attained his present high position, a boy entering college was recommended to his consideration.

"Try to draw the boy out, Professor; criticise him, and tell us what you think," the parents said.

To facilitate acquaintance the Professor took the boy for a walk. After ten minutes' silence the youth ventured: "Fine day, Professor."

"Yes," with a far-away look.

Ten minutes more, and the young man, squirming uncomfortably, said: "This is a pleasant walk, Professor."

"Yes."

Another silence, and then the young man blurted out that he thought they might have rain.

"Yes," and this time the Professor went on saying, "Young man, we have been walking together for half an hour, and you have said nothing which was not commonplace and stupid."

"Yes," said the boy, his irritation getting the better of his modesty, "and you endorsed every word I said."

Word from the Professor to the parents was to the effect that the boy was all right.

*****

A dear old citizen went to the cars the other day to see his daughter off on a journey. Securing her a seat he passed out of the car and went around to the car window to say a last parting word. While he was leaving the car the daughter crossed the aisle to speak to a friend, and at the same time a grim old maid took the seat and moved up to the window.

Unaware of the change the old gentleman hurriedly put his head up to the window and said: "One more kiss, pet."

In another instant the point of a cotton umbrella was thrust from the window, followed by the wrathful injunction: "Scat, you gray-headed wretch!"

* * * * *

There is a young physician who has never been able to smoke a cigar. "Just one poisons me," says the youthful doctor.

Recently the doctor was invited to a large dinner-party. When the women had left the table cigars were accepted by all the men except the physician. Seeing his friend refuse the cigar the host in astonishment exclaimed:

"What, not smoking? Why, my dear fellow, you lose half your dinner!"

"Yes, I know I do," meekly replied the doctor, "but if I smoked one I should lose the whole of it!"

* * * * *

Once, when Dr. Oliver Wendell Holmes was at a charitable fair, he was asked to furnish a letter for the "post-office." So he placed a one-dollar note inside a sheet of paper and wrote on the first page:

> "Dear lady, whosoe'er thou art,
> Turn this poor page with trembling care;
> But hush, oh, hush, thy beating heart,
> The one thou lov'st best will be there."

When the page was turned the one-dollar bill was revealed, and on the second page he wrote this verse:

> "Fair lady, lift thine eyes and tell
> If this is not a truthful letter;
> This is the 'one' thou lovest well,
> And naught (0) would make thee love it better."

* * * * *

As several travelers got into the station 'bus one of the men (who was quite a portly fellow) noticed that a certain young woman had a grip exactly like his, but that it was placed with the rest of the luggage, on top. Thinking there might be some mistake made he kept his inside and placed it at his feet. He was soon engrossed in his paper, and did not notice the young woman reach over and draw the grip close to her side. Being of a humorous turn of mind he waited until she was occupied with a book and then pulled the grip to its former position, the rest of the travelers looking on with amused expressions.

In turning over a leaf she looked down and suddenly became aware of the removal of the grip. She was quite indignant, and with some force in her voice and manner said, "That is *mine*!" and jerked it back close to her feet.

Touching his hat politely the owner said, with a merry twinkle in his eye: "All right, madam; but may I please get my pipe and nightshirt out? You are welcome to the rest of the things!"

* * * * *

President Eliot, of Harvard, is not a believer in spelling reform. Not long ago there was a student who was a candidate for the degree of doctor of philosophy.

This student had adopted spelling reform as his particular line of work, and as commencement day drew near he went to President Eliot with a request. "You know, Mr. President," he said "that you are proposing to make me a Ph.D. Now I have made a specialty of spelling reform and I always spell philosophy with an 'f.' I therefore called to ask you if you could not make my degree F. D., instead of Ph.D."

"Certainly," replied the President. "In fact, if you insist, we shall make it a D. F."

* * * * *

The following letter was received by the Post-office Department. It came from a Western postmaster at a small office and read: "In accordance with the rules of the department, I write you to inform you that on next Saturday I will close the post-office for one day, as I am going on a bear hunt. I am not asking your permission to close up and don't give a damn if you discharge me; but I will advise now, that I am the only man in the county who can read and write."

* * * * *

A young lady at a summer hotel asked an artist friend, who was spending his vacation there, if he would mind doing a small favor for her.

"Certainly not," he said eagerly; "what is it?"

"Thank you so much," she exclaimed gratefully. "I wish you would stop at Mrs. Gannon's little shop and get three large bone buttons, the kind with two small holes in them. They're for my new bathing suit, you know. Just tell her who I am and it will be all right. You needn't pay for them."

Now the artist was a bachelor, and had never bought anything but collar buttons before. So on the way to the store he kept repeating the instructions that he had received. Eager to relieve his mind he rushed up to Mrs. Gannon and reeled off this surprising speech: "I want three bone buttons for a small bathing suit with two large holes in it. Just tell me who I am and it will be all right."

* * * * *

There was not even standing room in the six-o'clock crowded car, but one more passenger, a young woman, wedged her way along just inside the doorway. Each time the car took a sudden lurch forward she fell helplessly back, and three times she landed in the arms of a large, comfortable man on the back platform. The third time it happened he said quietly: "Hadn't you better stay here now?"

* * * * *

The principal of one of Washington's high schools relates an incident in connection with the last commencement day. A clever girl had taken one of the principal prizes. At the close of the exercises her friends crowded about her to offer congratulations.

"Weren't you awfully afraid you wouldn't get it, Hattie?" asked one, "when there were so many contestants?"

"Oh, no!" cheerily exclaimed Hattie. "Because I knew when it came to English composition I had 'em all skinned."

* * * * *

The Guards' Band was playing on the terrace at Windsor Castle during luncheon, and the Queen was so pleased with a lively march that she sent a maid of honor to inquire what it was. The maid of honor blushed deeply as she answered on her return: "'Come where the Booze is Cheaper,' your Majesty."

* * * * *

Mark Twain once wrote to Andrew Carnegie as follows:

> "*My dear Mr. Carnegie:* I see by the papers that you are very prosperous. I want to get a hymn-book. It costs two dollars. I will bless you, God will bless you, and it will do a great deal of good. Yours truly, Mark Twain."

> "P. S.—Don't send the hymn-book; send me the two dollars."

* * * * *

A physician started a model insane asylum, says the New York "Sun," and set apart one ward especially for crazy motorists and chauffeurs. Taking a friend through the building he pointed out with particular pride the automobile ward and called attention to its elegant furnishings and equipment.

"But," said the friend, "the place is empty; I don't see any patients."

"Oh, they are all under the cots fixing the slats," explained the physician.

* * * * *

An aged, gray-haired and very wrinkled old woman, arrayed in the outlandish calico costume of the mountains, was summoned as a witness in court to tell what she knew about a fight in her house. She took the witness-stand with evidences of backwardness and proverbial Bourbon verdancy. The Judge asked her in a kindly voice what took place. She insisted it did not amount to much, but the Judge by his persistency finally got her to tell the story of the bloody fracas.

"Now, I tell ye, Jedge, it didn't amount to nuthn'. The fust I knowed about it was when Bill Saunder called Tom Smith a liar, en Tom knocked him down with a stick o' wood. One o' Bill's friends then cut Tom with a knife, slicin' a big chunk out o' him. Then Sam Jones, who was a friend of Tom's, shot the other feller and two more shot him, en three or four others got cut right smart by somebody. That nachly caused some excitement, Jedge, en then they commenced fightin'."

* * * * *

One morning, as Mr. Clemens returned from a neighborhood call, sans necktie, his wife met him at the door with the exclamation: "There, Sam, you have been over to the Stowes's again without a necktie! It's really disgraceful the way you neglect your dress!"

Her husband said nothing, but went up to his room.

A few minutes later his neighbor—Mrs. S.—was summoned to the door by a messenger, who presented her with a small box neatly done up. She opened it and found a black silk necktie, accompanied by the following note: "Here is a necktie. Take it out and look at it. I think I stayed half an hour this morning. At the end of that time will you kindly return it, as it is the only one I have?—MARK TWAIN."

* * * * *

The teacher was teaching a class in the infant Sabbath-school room and was making her pupils finish each sentence to show that they understood her.

"The idol had eyes," the teacher said, "but it could not—"

"See," cried the children.

"It had ears, but it could not—"

"Hear," was the answer.

"It had lips," she said, "but it could not—"

"Speak," once more replied the children.

"It had a nose, but it could not—"

"Wipe it," shouted the children; and the lesson had to stop a moment.

* * * * *

She was the dearest and most affectionate little woman in the world, and so thoughtful of her husband's comfort and his needs. One evening, when company was expected, she inquired solicitously:

"Aren't you going to wear that necktie I gave you on Christmas, dearie?"

"Of course I am, Henrietta," responded dearie. "I was saving it up. I am going to wear that red necktie, and my Nile-green smoking-jacket, and my purple and yellow socks, and open that box of cigars you gave me, all at once—to-night."

* * * * *

When J. M. Barrie addressed an audience of one thousand girls at Smith College during an American visit, a friend asked him how he had found the experience.

"Well," replied Mr. Barrie, "to tell you the truth I'd much rather talk one thousand times to one girl than to talk one time to a thousand girls."

* * * * *

The Rev. Mr. Goodman (inspecting himself in mirror)—"Caroline, I don't really believe I ought to wear this wig. It looks like living a lie."

"Bless your heart, Avery," said his better half, "don't let that trouble you. That wig will never fool anybody for one moment."

* * * * *

A young man had been calling now and then on a young lady, when one night as he sat in the parlor waiting for her to come down, her mother entered the room instead and asked in a grave, stern way what his intentions were. He was about to stammer a reply, when suddenly the young lady called down from the head of the stairs, "Oh, mama, that isn't the one."

* * * * *

A woman hurried up to a policeman at the corner of Twenty-third Street in New York City.

"Does this crosstown car take you down to the Bridge toward Brooklyn?" she demanded.

"Why, madam," returned the policeman, "do you want to go to Brooklyn?"

"No, I don't want to," the woman replied, "but I have to."

* * * * *

Walter Appleton Clark, whose artistic career was cut short by an untimely death, had a strong sense of humor. In going through a millionaire's stables, where the floors and walls were of white tiles, drinking fountains of marble, mahogany mangers, silver trimmings, and so forth and so on, "Well," said the millionaire proudly, "is there anything lacking?" "I can think of nothing," said Clark, "except a sofa for each horse."

* * * * *

Oliver Herford, equally famous as poet, illustrator, and brilliant wit, was entertaining four magazine editors at luncheon when the bell rang, and a maid entered with the mail.

"Oh," said an editor, "an epistle."

"No," said Mr. Herford, tearing open the envelope, "not an epistle, a collect."

* * * * *

An old gentleman on board one of the numerous steamers which ply between Holyhead and the Irish coast missed his handkerchief, and accused a soldier standing by his side of stealing it, which the soldier, an Irishman, denied. Some few minutes afterward the gentleman found the missing article in his hat; he was then most profuse in his apologies to the soldier.

"Not another wurrd," said Pat; "it was a misthake on both sides—ye took me for a thafe, and I took ye for a gintlemon."

* * * * *

The family were gathered in the library enjoying a magnificent thunder-storm when the mother thought of Dorothy alone in the nursery. Fearing lest the little daughter should be awakened and feel afraid, she slipped away to quiet her. Pausing at the door, however, in a vivid flash of lightning that illuminated the whole room, she saw the little girl sitting up in bed clapping her hands in excitement and shouting, "Bang it again, God! Bang it again!"

* * * * *

A little girl ate at a feast a great quantity of chocolate eggs and bananas and cakes and peanuts and things of that sort, and finally the time came for her to go.

"But you will have a little more cake before you go?" her hostess said politely.

"No, thank you, ma'am. I'm full," said the little girl.

"Then," said the hostess, "you'll put some nuts and candies in your pockets, won't you?"

The little girl shook her head regretfully.

"They're full, too," she said.

* * * * *

"My dear, I couldn't match that dress goods."

"You couldn't?"

"No, and after what the various clerks said to me, I can't see why a person in tolerable circumstances should want to match it."

* * * * *

A boy in a certain school would persist in saying "have went." One day the teacher kept him in, saying, "While I am out of the room you may write 'have gone' fifty times." When the teacher returned she found he had dutifully performed the task, but on the other side of the paper was a message from the absent one: "I have went. John White."

* * * * *

On one of his trips abroad Mr. Evarts landed at Liverpool. The steamer was proceeding slowly up the river to the wharf, and Mr. Evarts, after looking at the muddy waters of the Mersey, said to his companion, "Evidently the quality of mercy is not strained."

* * * * *

Once, at breakfast at a friend's, Phillips Brooks noticed the diminutive but amusingly dignified daughter of the house having constant trouble with the large fork that she was vainly trying to handle properly with her tiny fingers. In a spirit of kindness, mingled with mischief, the Bishop said:

"Why don't you give up the fork, my dear, and use your fingers? You know, fingers were made before forks."

Quick as a flash came the crushing retort: "Mine weren't."

* * * * *

Two stout old Germans were enjoying their pipes and placidly listening to the strains of the summer-garden orchestra. One of them in tipping his chair back stepped on a parlor match, which exploded with a bang.

"Dot vas not on de program," he said, turning to his companion.

"Vat was not?"

"Vy, dot match."

"Vat match?"

"De match I valked on."

"Vell, I didn't see no match; vat aboud it?"

"Vy, I valked on a match and it vent bang, and I said it vas not on de program."

The other picked up his program and read it through very carefully. "I don't see it on de program," he said.

"Vell, I said it vas not on the program, didn't I?"

"Vell, vat has it got to do mit de program, anyvay? Egsplain yourself."

* * * * *

Charles Dana Gibson, the creator of the "Gibson girl," is one of the tallest men in his profession, standing six feet two inches tall and weighing two hundred pounds.

A fellow-illustrator, called upon Mr. Gibson in his studio one day and found him working at a specially constructed table accommodated to his height and breadth. He shook hands cordially with his visitor, but his frank face revealed deep discontent. His visitor expressed the fear that his visit was untimely.

"Not at all, my dear fellow," Mr. Gibson responded. "But I was just looking at this as you came in," and he showed him a very small pen, called a crow-quill, with which illustrators make their sketches. The crow-quill is smaller than the ordinary pen and holder, a fragile, perishable, and insignificant instrument.

"Just look at it," complained Mr. Gibson, "and think of a man of my size earning his living with a thing like that!"

* * * * *

Going into a port where the water was very deep—Rio de Janeiro, I believe—relates Captain A. T. Mahan, the chain cables "got away," as the expression is, control was lost, and shackle after shackle tore out of the hawse-holes with tremendous rattling and roaring. The admiral was on deck at the moment, and when the chain had been stopped and secured he said to the captain: "Alfred, send for the young man in charge of those chains and give him a good setting-down. Ask him what he means by letting such things happen." Alfred was a mild person, and clearly did not like his job; he could not have come up to the admiral's standard. The latter saw it, and said: "Perhaps you had better leave it to me. I'll settle him." Fixing his eyes on the offender, he said, sternly: "What do you mean by this, sir? Why the hell didn't you stop that chain?" The culprit looked quietly at him and said: "How the hell could I?" After a moment the admiral turned to the captain and said meekly: "That's true, Alfred; how the hell could he?"

* * * * *

An old darky of the Blue Grass State was looking at the high steppers belonging to his new master, who said, "I suppose your master down South had a good many horses?" "'Deed we did, sah, dat we did; an' ole massa had 'em all name' Bible names. Faith, Hope, and Charity, Bustle, Stays, and Crinoline was all one spring's colts!"

* * * * *

The wife of a well-known judge lost her cook, and since she had no other re-course she rolled up her sleeves and for a week provided such meals as the judge had not enjoyed since those happy days when they didn't keep a cook. The judge's delight was so great that by way of acknowledgment he presented his wife with a beautiful ermine coat. Naturally the incident was noised about among their acquaintances and a spirit of envious emulation was developed in certain quarters. Mrs. Jerome, after reciting the story to her husband, asked, "What do I get, Jerry, if I will do the cooking for a week?"

"At the end of the week, dear, you'll get one of those long crêpe veils."

* * * * *

Perhaps one of Lord Beaconsfield's brightest flings was at the wife of his bitterest political foe. Mrs. Gladstone passed the Prime Minister one day, and he cast a glance at her over his shoulder, saying: "There goes a woman without one redeeming fault."

* * * * *

A private, anxious to secure leave of absence, sought his captain with a most convincing tale about a sick wife breaking her heart for his presence.

The officer, familiar with the soldier's ways, replied:

"I am afraid you are not telling the truth. I have just received a letter from your wife urging me not to let you come home because you get drunk, and mistreat her shamefully."

The private saluted and started to leave the room. He paused at the door, asking: "Sor, may I spake to you, not as an officer, but as mon to mon?"

"Yes, what is it?"

"You and I are two of the most illigant liars the Lord ever made. I'm not married at all."

* * * * *

A very prosy gentleman, who was in the habit of waylaying Douglas Jerrold, met his victim and, planting himself in the way, said: "Well, Jerrold, what is going on to-day?"

Jerrold replied, darting past the inquirer, "I am!"

* * * * *

Foote, the English actor, was once praising the hospitality of the Irish, after one of his trips to Ireland. A gentleman in his audience asked him whether he had ever been at Cork. "No, sir," replied Foote; "but I have seen many drawings of it."

* * * * *

A lady one day meeting a girl who had formerly been in her employ inquired,

"Well Mary, where do you live now?" "Please ma'am, I don't live nowhere now," rejoined the girl; "I am married."

* * * * *

When a Mr. Wilberforce was a candidate for election in Hull, England, his sister, an amiable and witty young lady offered to make a present of a new gown to each of the wives of the men who voted for her brother. Upon hearing this, the crowd whom she was addressing broke out into cries of "Miss Wilberforce forever." "I thank you gentlemen," the young lady replied, "but I do not wish to be Miss Wilberforce forever!"

* * * * *

"How do you define 'black as your hat?'" said a schoolmaster to one of his pupils.

"Darkness that may be felt," replied the budding genius.

* * * * *

She—"He married her for her money. Wasn't that awful?"

He—"Did he get it?"

She—"No."

He—"It was."

* * * * *

"My, but it is hot in your office," said a client to his lawyer.

"It ought to be," replied the lawyer, "I make my bread here."

* * * * *

The town council of a small German community met to inspect a new site for a cemetery. They assembled at a chapel, and as it was a warm day some one suggested they leave their coats there.

"Some one can stay behind and watch them," suggested Herr Botteles.

"What for?" demanded Herr Ehrlich. "If we are all going out together what need is there for any one to watch the clothes?"

* * * * *

After a brief two weeks' acquaintance he invited her to go to the ball-game with him.

"There's Jarvis! He's a good one. He's a pitcher for your life. And that's Johnson, over there. He's going to be our best man in a few weeks."

"Oh, Walter! He'll do, all right," she lisped hurriedly, "but it is so sudden, dear."

* * * * *

Dr. Edward Waldo Emerson, of Concord, is fond of telling of an old servant whose heart was exceedingly kind, and in whom the qualities of pity and compassion were developed nearly to perfection. He was once driving his master and Emerson through the country. As they approached a new house that the master was building, they saw an old woman sneaking away with a bundle of wood. "Jabez, Jabez," cried the master, "do you see that old woman taking my wood?" Jabez looked with pity at the old woman, then with scorn at his master. "No, sir," he said stoutly, "I don't see her, and I didn't think that you would see her either."

* * * * *

"They said that we would never be happy," moaned the young bride.

"But you *are* happy."

"But now they say it won't last."

* * * * *

"That fellow," said Alfred Henry Lewis, the other day, when a certain well-known Tammany man was mentioned, "puts up a good bluff, but there is nothing to him. Open the front door and you are in his back yard."

* * * * *

Little Paul trying on his grandmother's glasses—"Grandma, what is it between my eyes and the glasses, I can't see anything."

"Eighty years, my dear."

* * * * *

To Richard Mansfield an enthusiastic woman admirer had paid tribute of praise, adding: "I suppose, sir, that when in the spirit of those great rôles you forget your real self for days."

"Yes, madam, for days, as well as nights. It is then I do those dreadful things— trample on the upturned features of my leading lady and hurl tenderloin steaks at waiters."

"And you do not know of it at all?"

"Not a solitary thing, until I read the papers the next day," said Mr. Mansfield solemnly.

* * * * *

When Marquis Ito was in the United States, in 1901, an inexperienced St. Paul reporter sought an interview with him. He met Ito's secretary, and made known his mission. "Me newspaper man. Me writee news. Me heardee marquis velly ill. He better to-day? You savve?" began the reporter, to the secretary's amazement. But the latter was equal to the occasion. "Me savve," he said gravely. "Marquis he no better. Belly blad. Catchee cold. Doctor him no lettee him leave bled to-day. You savve?" The interview proceeded in this way, but at its termination the secretary, with a twinkle in his eye, remarked: "The marquis is greatly fatigued by his arduous journey, but—" But the reporter had fled.

* * * * *

Professor Phelps, who disliked mathematics, was once walking with Professor

Newton, who began discussing a problem so deep that his companion could not follow it. He fell into a brown study, from which he was aroused by Newton's emphatic assertion, "And that, you see, gives us x!" "Does it?" asked Mr. Phelps, politely. "Why, doesn't it?" exclaimed the professor, excitedly, alarmed at the possibility of a flaw in his calculations. Quickly his mind ran back and detected a mistake. "You are right, Mr. Phelps. You are right!" shouted the professor. "It doesn't give us x; it gives us y." And from that time Professor Phelps was looked upon as a mathematical prodigy, the first man who ever tripped Newton.

* * * * *

Ambassador Choate and his daughter visited the restaurant made famous by Dr. Samuel Johnson. It is the custom there to give the guests lark pie, such as Johnson used to eat, and the Choates were served with one of the pasties. Choate was in the chair that Johnson was wont to occupy, and had just begun his meal, when his daughter exclaimed: "Isn't it funny, papa? You are in Johnson's chair and eating a tradition." "Eating a tradition!" retorted the ambassador struggling valiantly; "I have got hold of one of Johnson's larks."

* * * * *

A New England school-teacher recited "The Landing of the Pilgrims" to her pupils, then asked each of them to draw from their imagination a picture of Plymouth Rock. One little fellow hesitated and then raised his hand. "Well, Willie, what is it?" asked the teacher. "Please teacher, do you want us to draw a hen or a rooster?"

* * * * *

An English gentleman had sent a private note to a marquis, on a personal matter, by hand, and on the return of the man questioned him as to his reception. "Ah, sir," said the man, "there's no use writing him any letter, he can't see to read them. He's blind."

"Blind!"

"Yes, sir. He asked me twice where my hat was, and I had it on my head all the time."

* * * * *

A magician was performing in a Kentucky town, and during the evening announced that in his next trick he would need a pint flask of whisky. No move was made to supply the liquor. "Perhaps you did not understand me. Will some gentleman kindly loan me a pint flask of whisky?" Then a lank man in the rear of the hall arose. "Mistah," said he, "will a quart flask do?" "Just as well, sir," replied the magician, and every gentleman in the hall arose with flask extended.

* * * * *

"Phœbe," said a mistress in reproof to her colored servant whom she found smoking a short pipe after having repeatedly threatened to discharge her if again caught in the act, "if you won't stop that bad habit for any other reason do so because it is right. You are a good church member—and, don't you know that smoking makes the breath unpleasant, and that nothing unclean can enter Heaven?" "'Deed, missie, I does," said the woman, "but bress' yo' heart, when I go to Heaben I'll leave my bref behin'."

* * * * *

It was the custom of a certain deacon, when dining at the home of one of his best friends, to drink a glass of milk, as a prelude to his dinner. One day when the minister was scheduled to appear, instead of the rich, foamy glass of milk, his friend placed beside his plate a glass of milk punch. After the blessing, the deacon seized his glass and drank to the last drop, and then exclaimed as he closed his eyes and smacked his lips, "*Oh*, what a cow!"

* * * * *

Dean Hole of Rochester, England, told of a very innocent and obliging curate who went to a Yorkshire parish where many of the parishioners bred horses and sometimes raced them. A few Sundays after his arrival he was asked to invite the prayers of the congregation for Lucy Grey. He did so. They prayed for three Sundays for her. On the fourth, the church clerk told the curate that he need not do it any more. "Why," he asked, "is she dead?" "No," said the clerk, "she's won the steeplechase."

* * * * *

The late Richard Henry Stoddard while endeavoring to procure an impromptu luncheon for a number of his friends after his wife and the servants had retired, found a box of sardines. His vigorous remarks, inspired by the sardine-can's objections to the "open sesame" of a dull jack-knife, attracted the attention of Mrs. Stoddard on the floor above.

"What *are* you doing?" she called down.

"Opening a can of sardines."

"With what?"

"A dashed old jack-knife," cried the exasperated poet; "what did you think I was opening it with?"

"Well, dear," she answered, "I didn't think you were opening it with prayer."

* * * * *

"What is the matter with your father, Gladys?" asked the child's aunt.

"He's awful sick with a headache," the little girl answered, "an' he's hurt, too, 'cause mama said he's broke his resolution."

* * * * *

Colored people are proverbially fond of funerals, and Mrs. Walker's cook was trying to make her mistress realize what she had missed by not attending the funeral of a prominent citizen of their village.

"Mis' Fanny," she said, "you sholy orto hev been thar. I ain' nevvah seen sech a big funril in dis heah town. Dey had all de kerridges fum bofe liberty stables, 'mos' all de private conveniences, an' dat new fambly fum de North was dere in a two-hoss syringe!"

* * * * *

William Bourke Cochran took his seat in Congress on the day that the House went into turmoil over the special report on post-office affairs. "I suppose it looks like old times to you, Cochran," said a friend, who, with others, had crowded around to welcome him back. Just then such epithets as "coward," "knave," "scoundrel," and "liar," hurtled across the chamber. "Well, I can't say it looks much like old times," replied Cochran, "too many new faces for that. But it certainly sounds like old times."

* * * * *

This happened in Scotland: The last edition of the newspapers had been sold out and the newsboys were calculating their takings. "Hallo," said Jimmy, in alarm, "I'm a 'a'penny short!" "Well, wats the use of 'arpin' on it?" growled Dick, as he calmly cracked a nut; "you don't think I took it, do you?" "I don't say you 'ave. But there it is, I'm a 'a'penny short, and you're eatin' nuts."

* * * * *

In *the* "Diary of a Frenchman" by Flandrau, he makes a student say to his chum: "I've an idea that we're going to have 'je suis bon' in French to-day. I wish you would write out a few tenses for me."

Whereupon his friend wrote:

> "Je suis bon.
> Tu es bones,
> Il est beans,
> Nous sommes bon bons,
> Vous êtes bonbonnières,
> Ils sont bon-ton."

* * * * *

Tolstoy told Isabel Habgard, who has translated many of his books, a good story of one of his ancestors, an army officer, who was an excellent mimic. One day he was impersonating the Emperor Paul to a group of his friends, when Paul himself entered, and for some moments looked on, unperceived, at the antics of the young man. Tolstoy finally turned, and beholding the emperor, bowed his head and was silent. "Go on, sir," said Paul; "continue the performance." The young man hesitated a moment, and then, folding his arms and imitating every gesture and intonation of his sovereign, he said: "Tolstoy, you deserve to be degraded, but I remember the thoughtlessness of youth, and you are pardoned." The czar smiling, said, "Well, be it so."

* * * * *

When President Nicholas Murray Butler was at college, certain freshmen of his time made no scruple of stealing a pail of milk which a dairyman daily placed outside the door of Mr. Butler's room while the occupant was in class. In order to foil the boys, Mr. Butler printed a sign in big letters, "I have poisoned this milk with arsenic." Upon his return he found the milk intact, but added to the notice were these words: "So have we."

* * * * *

There is an amusing story told of a clergyman, who, upon one of his trips through the West, observed that almost every man he met and spoke with used profanity. Finally he found one man who talked to him for twenty minutes without using an oath. The clergyman shook hands with him at parting and said: "You don't know how glad I am to have a chance to have a talk with a man like you. You are the first man I have met for three days who could talk for five minutes without swearing." The stranger, shocked, instantly and innocently ejaculated: "Well, I'll be d——d!"

* * * * *

The other day, while shopping, a lady accidentally picked up another lady's umbrella from the counter, and had the mistake pointed out to her in a rather frigid manner. She returned the umbrella with apologies, and then remembered that she had no umbrella with her.

As it had begun to rain, she bought one, as well as one for a birthday present for a friend. With the two umbrellas in her hand, she boarded a car and, as luck would have it, sat down opposite the lady whose umbrella she had picked up earlier in the store. As the latter swept out of the car she smiled again frigidly, and remarked to the lady of the umbrellas, "I see you have had a successful day."

* * * * *

"If a fairy should appear to you and offer you three wishes," said the imaginative young woman, "what would you do?" "I'd sign the pledge," answered the matter-of-fact young man.

* * * * *

A summer tourist was passing through a German village in the West recently, when a stout German girl came to the front door and called to a small girl playing in front. "Gusty! Gusty!" she said, "come in and eat yourself. Ma's on the table, and pa's half et!"

* * * * *

A university of Illinois professor is very popular among the students. He was entertaining a group of them at his residence one night. Taking down a magnificent sword that hung over the fireplace, he brandished it about, exclaiming, "Never will I forget the day I drew this blade for the first time." "Where did you draw it, sir?" an awe-struck freshman asked. "At a raffle," said the professor.

* * * * *

In the vicinity of Germantown there lived a worthy old lady and her son John, who were once called upon to entertain a number of ladies at dinner during Quarterly meeting. As John began to carve the broiled chickens, he entered upon a flowery speech of welcome, but in the midst of his flattering utterances his mother, who was somewhat deaf, piped up from the other end of the table: "You needn't be praisin' of 'em up, John, I'm afraid they're a lot of tough old hens, every one of 'em."

* * * * *

One of Père Ollivier's flock, a very beautiful and handsomely dressed woman, coming very late to church one Sunday morning, caused some disturbance and stir among the worshipers by her entrance and interrupted the flow of eloquence of the worthy father, who, very irritable and easily put out, said: "Madame perhaps waited to take her chocolate before coming to church?" To this, madame, unabashed, graciously replied: "Yes, mon père; and two rolls with it."

* * * * *

Of late years the House of Commons has seen some lively times. Many of them have been brought about by the irascible but delightful Irish member, Dr. Tanner. On one occasion, when he had been indulging rather freely and his ever ready tongue being loosened, he met Sir Ellis Ashmead Bartlett in the lobby, and taking him to one side he said, in the greatest confidence, and without the slightest tinge of anger, but with a world of meaning: "Bartlett, you are a fool." "You are drunk," retorted the knight. "That's all right," replied Dr. Tanner. "To-morrow I shall be sober, but you will still be a fool."

* * * * *

A reader for a New York publishing house gives the following, quoted from a story submitted by an Indiana authoress, as being about the choicest bit he has come across in many years:

> "Reginald was bewitched. Never had the baroness seemed to
> him so beautiful as at this moment, when, in her dumb grief, she
> hid her face."

* * * * *

An old negro living in Carrollton was taken ill recently, and called in a physician of his race to prescribe for him. But the old man did not seem to be getting any better, and finally a white physician was called. Soon after arriving Dr. S—— felt the darky's pulse for a moment, and then examined his tongue. "Did your other doctor take your temperature?" he asked. "I don't know, sah," he answered, feebly; "I haint missed nuthin' but mah watch yit, boss."

Lector House believes that a society develops through a two-fold approach of continuous learning and adaptation, which is derived from the study of classic literary works spread across the historic timeline of literature records. Therefore, we aim at reviving, repairing and redeveloping all those inaccessible or damaged but historically as well as culturally important literature across subjects so that the future generations may have an opportunity to study and learn from past works to embark upon a journey of creating a better future.

This book is a result of an effort made by Lector House towards making a contribution to the preservation and repair of original ancient works which might hold historical significance to the approach of continuous learning across subjects.

HAPPY READING & LEARNING!

LECTOR HOUSE LLP
E-MAIL: lectorpublishing@gmail.com